THE *SUPERPOWER* OF SELF-CONFIDENCE FOR TEENS

DISCOVER THE SECRET WEAPON TO CONQUER FEAR, OVERCOME INSECURITY, AND DEFEAT LOW SELF-ESTEEM

ROBIN ROTH

CONTENTS

INTRODUCTION

Your teenage years are meant to be one of the most memorable and enjoyable periods of your life. The youthful energy, the excitement of becoming a young adult, and the adventure of discovering what matters to you and how you want to live your life make being a teenager a wholly unique and transformative time in your life. Some of the choices we make as teenagers can impact the trajectory of our lives and many of our experiences affect the way we view ourselves, others, and the world. In order to make the most of your teenage years, it's important to prepare yourself for any challenges you may face on your journey so you can live joyfully and grow into the person you are meant to be.

Life has inevitable ups and downs, but you can find a way to persevere and overcome any obstacles that may arise.

Because of the many changes all teens go through during this unique time, you may find yourself facing challenges and adversity you've never encountered before, but you have it within you to face those hardships and move past them. Adolescence is a time for young people to explore their identities in order to become the best and most authentic versions of themselves, but it's not always easy. The teenage years can also bring inner turmoil, uncertainty, and conflict in relationships. You want to prepare for these challenges so you can handle them confidently and continue growing as an individual.

Sometimes, people who feel they aren't achieving their goals or fulfilling their potential may turn their inner disappointment outward, projecting their anger and negativity onto others. For example, someone who struggles in school or doesn't put in their total effort may give those who do a hard time, try to make them feel bad about themselves, or even try to pressure them into doing their work for them. Someone who struggles with their self-esteem may find themselves the target of this type of bully and may be at risk of feeling bad about themselves and who they are. When bullies are hurting and don't like themselves, their coping mechanism is often to project their pain and shame onto other people. It hurts them to see others happy and doing well when they feel inadequate, insecure, or hopeless. Sadly, when they see someone else hurting as they are, it makes them feel better. This can result in a toxic cycle where the bully never really addresses their real issues, and the victim starts to believe there may be something inherently wrong with them.

Understanding why bullies try to inflict pain on others and how to protect yourself from their negativity can equip you with the knowledge and tools you need to create happy memories during your teenage years and a strong foundation for the rest of your life. Social relationships and interactions have a significant impact on teens' mental health. It can feel suffocating if you live in an environment where you feel self-conscious or are frequently targeted by bullies and don't have the space to be yourself freely. It becomes even harder when you feel like you are the only one having difficulty fitting in with others. Life can start to feel very lonely when you don't feel accepted or that you have a place in the world.

What's even more heartbreaking is when you are not around the bullies but still feel like you are inadequate, ugly, or unlovable. It's devastating to look at yourself in the mirror and realize that you doubt yourself and have lost faith in your worth and true identity. Adolescence is a time when you are trying to find answers about what truly defines you and what your purpose is, but only you can determine the answers to those questions. Though it can be hard, you should never allow others—whether they be friends, family members, bullies, or society as a whole —to tell you who you are or who you should be. You may sometimes feel that you are not capable of attaining your dreams or that you aren't good enough, and often bullies will try to reinforce these insecurities because it makes them feel powerful and in control. You may struggle to block out negativity, but that can change if you take the right steps toward living the life you truly deserve. You shouldn't take the hurtful things others, and maybe even yourself, say about who you are to heart; instead, focus on the truth about how wonderful and capable you really are and how you have the ability to create the life you want for yourself. Hold onto that truth and carry it with you for the rest of your life.

Maybe you're not convinced and you're thinking, *But I don't even know the truth about who I am, and that is why I end up doubting myself and believing the negative things people say about me...* If this sounds familiar, then you are in the right place, and I'm so glad you're here. This book will walk through all those worries swirling in your head. Together, we will dismantle any limiting beliefs you may have about yourself, realize how wrong they are, and silence any negative self-talk that may be keeping you from the life you want to live.

You deserve to not only enjoy your teenage years but to live a happy, fulfilled, and successful life. You have the power to overcome any negativity that has been holding you back from expressing yourself freely, creating the relationships you want, and going after your dreams. On this journey, you will gain an understanding of many of the struggles teens face as they work to develop their confidence and self-identity. You will also learn practical tools to help you say goodbye to the old version of yourself and unlock the door for the new confident, self-assured, and unstoppable version.

If you're unsure that you have the ability to make these changes, realize that that is just a symptom of the low self-esteem we will work on improving. Those negative beliefs come from a vulnerable place and a mindset that holds no truth and does you no favors. We are here to reverse those thoughts and show you how to change your thought processes. Once you start developing a growth mindset and unshakable confidence, your thoughts, beliefs, and self-talk will also transform to fit that new reality.

Many people have already walked this road. My son was a victim of relentless bullying in school. It forced him to change schools three times. It caused him a great deal of heartache, anxiety, and depression. It affected me immensely to see his suffering, which has motivated me to reach out to others going through those same struggles. I deeply understand the anguish, desperation, and sorrow teens feel when facing adverse and painful circumstances. If he could overcome those struggles and become a successful and happy adult, you certainly can too! In fact, many celebrities most teens know and love didn't start out as confident and put-together as you see them today; they, too, had their rough patches and share of hardships. What made a difference in their lives and put a stop to those negative patterns was the work they put in to overcome and move past those challenges.

For instance, you've probably heard of Priyanka Chopra—she's Nick Jonas's wife and once won the Miss Universe crown. If you look at her level of success and confidence today, you might think she never experienced bullying or low self-esteem as a teen. However, she was, in fact, a victim of bullying and battled through a time in her life when the negative voice in her head made it hard for her to believe in herself and recognize and embrace the beauty she possessed inside and out. In an article published by *The News International,* she revealed a detailed account of her struggles when she came from India and started attending school in the United States. She shared about a girl who used to bully her and push her up against the lockers. The bully despised her for being liked by a guy that the girl liked. Imagine someone hating you just because someone else feels a certain way about you, making you feel bad about yourself and ashamed of who you are. Now imagine all the untold stories of hurt and sadness caused by being bullied that she carries in her heart, which eventually pushed her to go back to India for some time. Luckily, she never gave up on herself despite those moments of defeat and despair, and she eventually managed to restore her confidence and live a beautiful and successful life (Web Desk, 2023).

So many people have risen above their personal challenges and courageously stepped into the lives they envisioned for themselves. I know that you have this same ability within you! Now it's your turn to realize the depth of your own power—your Superpower—so you can build the life you envision for yourself by conquering your fears, overcoming your insecurities, and defeating low self-esteem. Embrace who you are and chase your dreams!

1

HOW TO UNLOCK YOUR CONFIDENCE

MOVE FROM DOUBT TO EMPOWERMENT

Believe in yourself! Have faith in your abilities! Without a humble but reasonable confidence in your own powers you cannot be successful or happy.

— NORMAN VINCENT PEALE

Confidence is undeniably one of the most alluring qualities anyone can have. However, what exactly does it mean to be someone who is confident? Let's start by breaking down the main facets of confidence.

A confident person is someone who genuinely believes in their worth, is comfortable with themself, and embraces who they are as an individual. Having confidence means you are not ashamed of yourself and that you have faith in your abilities; it means you are brave enough to stand up for yourself and be assertive. Being self-confident also means knowing what you're good at and being okay with what you can't do. A confident person is better prepared to deal with challenges and disappointments. Confidence doesn't prevent failure, but it does make you feel like you can overcome obstacles and move past them.

On the other hand, people who lack confidence often experience stress, depression, social anxiety, fear of rejection, and feelings of inferiority or unworthiness and can be prone to overthinking and people-pleasing tendencies. People who lack confidence may also downplay their achievements and exhibit poor performance in school, sports, or other activities, poor self-care habits, undefined boundaries, or have trouble asserting themselves. They may avoid social situations or new opportunities and struggle to establish or maintain healthy relationships. A lack of confidence can affect almost every aspect of someone's life and even make taking part in everyday activities feel daunting.

When you are confident, it's easier to take advantage of opportunities and connect with others because you are not afraid to explore the world and try new things. Confident people tend to attract friends and happiness, get great results from their efforts, and solve problems effectively.

However, without confidence, it's hard to feel lasting happiness and have a sense of belonging. You may start to experience what's known as "imposter syndrome." This is when you feel like you don't deserve the success or happiness you may be experiencing or working toward. You feel like a phony in your own life, constantly plagued by the fear of being unmasked and exposed as a fraud. Imposter syndrome occurs when you struggle to recognize your achievements or feel others are more deserving than you. This difficult phenomenon can trick you into believing you are less worthy than others and are not meant to experience success or contentment. You might have difficulty celebrating your achievements and may even choose to give up on things that are important to you, like school, friendships, or hobbies.

You might be thinking, *I'm so young, but why do I feel so bad about myself? Where did this lack of confidence come from?* The root cause of imposter syndrome has to do with childhood trauma. If you grew up in a family that had trouble communicating and showing or dealing with emotions, you might have trouble with relationships or even develop an insecure attachment style.

According to Verywell Mind, an insecure attachment style results in difficulty trusting others and feelings of not having a safe and secure foundation (Feuerman, 2022). It affects your relationships with others as well as yourself, causing you to mistrust others and doubt yourself. An insecure attachment style typically develops when a parent makes a child "pay" for being loved rather than showing the child unconditional love, causing feelings of insecurity in the child. Instead of freely being themselves and believing that they are worthy of love just for being who they are, children with an insecure attachment style feel like they have to act a certain way in order to receive love and have their needs met. For instance, if a parent only shows love and attention to their child when they do well in school or what the parent wants, it makes the child believe that they are unlovable when they fail in school or don't meet their parent's expectations. Instead of being secure and happy with who they are, children with an insecure attachment style start to feel very ashamed of the sides of themselves that their parents don't seem to love. They start to become people pleasers and lose the sense of independence they need as they grow up. Your growth shouldn't revolve around doing what your parents want; you should also have the liberty and confidence to have your own dreams, explore the world the way you want to, and be who you want to be. Parents should also give their children the room to be their unique selves and not who they think their children should be. Of course, parents should also do their best to guide their children in making good choices and provide logical consequences when boundaries are crossed.

A secure attachment style is also developed mainly as an outcome of the way someone was raised. If someone grew up with a parent who showed them love just for being who they are and embraced every side of them while also encouraging healthy growth and development as an individual, this would help the person become very secure and self-assured. Since their parents or caregivers showed them compassion, acceptance, and unconditional love, they will grow up mirroring that behavior and become someone who has self-compassion, self-love, and self-respect. Being encouraged to explore the world and learn as much as they can would also positively influence their confidence as they would develop the courage and curiosity to seek out new opportunities and experiences. However, if they were criticized and not supported whenever they tried to put themselves out there, play and be creative, or do new things, that would instill fear and self-doubt during their developmental stages.

To become confident, any damaging experiences you may have had during your early childhood years need to be addressed and resolved. So, if you think you might have an insecure attachment style, it's important to invest your time in learning how to develop a secure attachment style. This is where reparenting becomes crucial. Thankfully, by reparenting yourself, you can undergo a process of cognitive restructuring that allows you to shift the way you see yourself and others. Reparenting means giving your inner child what you always needed and wanted from your parents (Clarke, 2022). For example, if you wanted more affirmations that you are lovable, you would start telling yourself the things you longed to hear as a child.

It's important to acknowledge that most of the signs and symptoms of a lack of confidence indicate some form of childhood trauma; this empowers you to reframe your life by putting in place strategies that will help you start healing from those wounds. Being aware of the role your past plays in impacting your personality should not be used as a weapon of judgment toward those who raised you. Instead, it's important to remember that many caregivers sometimes hurt us without even knowing the effects of their actions. For the most part, parents and caregivers do the best they can with what they know. Think about it: If you were raised by a parent with an insecure attachment style, chances are they may not have even known how to build a healthy, secure relationship with you as a parent themself. Since they have difficulty forming secure attachments, all they could do was pass on to you what they knew based on how they were raised. Thus, having empathy toward those who raised us instead of blaming them for the low self-esteem we experience helps bring lasting healing to everyone.

So how exactly do people become secure and confident? Many people think confidence comes from being good at certain things or having a lot of friends, but in fact, a person can acknowledge their flaws or weaknesses and still be confident. The idea that someone has to be "perfect" before they can be confident is a misguided notion. As human beings, we are insatiable by nature, so no matter how much you accomplish, there will always be more you can strive for. Because of this, waiting until you've achieved one thing or another in order to feel like you can be confident is a mistake—you can be confident anytime you decide you want to be! Isn't that great news?

Many teens start to become aware of the things about themselves they are unhappy with or wish they could change. This awareness can quickly diminish your confidence, and the more you look for flaws, the more your confidence will go downhill. So, how do you maintain your confidence and help it grow even during this turbulent and sometimes difficult time in your life? Let's look at some ways you can start to reparent yourself and develop confidence and a secure attachment style.

HOW TO DEVELOP CONFIDENCE AND A SECURE ATTACHMENT STYLE

In order to develop lasting confidence, you'll first need to recognize and start to dismantle the thoughts and behaviors that come from an insecure attachment style. You can do this by observing how people with a secure attachment style interact in their relationships and using that as a model for your own behavior.

No matter what you experienced as a child, it is possible to overcome any adversity and reframe your mindset, and one way to start doing that is by using positive affirmations. Here are a few affirmations you can use to shift away from your insecurities and move toward building healthy relationships with yourself and others:

- I am beautiful/handsome the way I was created; things like my appearance, the things I have, or where I come from don't define my worth. I am priceless and beautiful no matter what.
- I am loved unconditionally. Despite being flawed in some ways, I am still worthy of love.
- My loved ones trust me and believe in me. More importantly, I believe and trust in myself. I have the freedom to discover what matters to me and to go after my dreams.
- I am not afraid of rejection because I fully accept myself.
- I don't need to put on a facade or be a people pleaser just to be liked. I want to be true to myself and live on my own terms.
- I will give and accept love freely.
- I do not need to depend on others in order to be happy or make sure my needs are met. I will maintain a healthy balance in my expectations of myself and others.

By being truthful with yourself and expressing your needs in healthy ways, you will start to become more grounded and happier in your relationships. It's hard to be confident about relationships founded on an insecure attachment style, including disorganized, avoidant, or ambivalent attachment styles. People with any of these types of insecure attachment styles struggle with their own confidence as well as in relationships. People with an avoidant attachment style may avoid getting close to others because they are afraid of getting hurt or being rejected. An ambivalent attachment style is seen in people who want to have relationships but struggle to put their trust in others and become overbearing or possessive. A disorganized insecure attachment style is characterized by difficulty with managing emotions and even somewhat distorted views of the world and other people (Feuerman, 2022). Any of these can cause a person to lack confidence in themself and their interpersonal relationships.

The solution to breaking free from this internal turmoil is to cultivate self-love and self-compassion. Once you love and respect yourself, you will begin to feel comfortable confidently expressing who you really are around others. Even if you encounter unkindness, rejection, or conflict, you can move past it because you can sufficiently meet your own needs. Once you become accustomed to thinking this way, people will start to take notice of the positive energy you project. Often, people who come across as "needy" seem to lack confidence; they may overextend themselves in their friendships or struggle with unreciprocated love in their romantic interests. This quality of neediness results from valuing others above yourself and may unintentionally send the message that you don't love yourself enough, which can further compound the cycle of rejection. This is why it's difficult to earn true acceptance and respect from others if you tend toward people-pleasing behaviors—people can sense that something is wrong and that you are hiding who you truly are.

The key to being self-assured and confident in yourself is to realize that the internal validation you give yourself is far more impactful than fleeting external validation. When you can give yourself what you are looking for from others, your inner love and acceptance will begin to shine through for everyone else to see.

Self-Confidence vs. Self-Esteem

Understanding the difference between self-confidence and self-esteem is extremely important because it can help you figure out the right action steps to take when you're struggling with one or the other. It's easy to confuse self-confidence and self-esteem because they seem so similar. Confidence means trusting that you have the ability to perform a certain role well. For instance, if you were a chef, you would most likely have confidence and trust in your ability to cook delicious food, or if you were an athlete who has been training for years, you would most likely have trust in your ability to compete well in your sport. On the other hand, self-esteem is how you value and love yourself. It includes what you think of yourself and your perception of how deserving you are to be respected and happy.

Many people will try to boost their self-esteem by doing things that will actually only boost their confidence.

Maybe you have met someone who is good at sports and school and has a lot of friends but still seems to think they're not good enough. People with low self-esteem often have a negative self-perception, which makes it hard for them to be happy no matter how much they might excel in certain areas of their life. It makes sense because external achievements won't permanently fill the internal void created by a lack of self-love and self-worth. Sometimes people with low self-esteem might start to feel really good about themselves as they become better at certain things, but true self-esteem requires more than just being good at things on the outside.

Perhaps you used to struggle in school but worked really hard to bring your grades up. This would definitely make you feel more confident, but you might still deal with feelings of low self-esteem. This is because external accomplishments only serve to boost our confidence instead of having the ability to sustainably change our self-esteem. Once you recognize this important distinction, you will be able to work on things that truly will boost your self-esteem, but it is possible to do both. You can strike a good balance by improving your confidence by becoming better at what you do as well as improving your self-esteem by working on your internal belief system.

Our self-esteem and confidence both have to be healthy if we are to truly feel happy and at ease with ourselves. If you have healthy self-esteem but low self-confidence, you may have trouble feeling good about yourself in areas like schoolwork, sports, friendships, and even eventually your career. Thus, you'll want to focus on learning the skills that will help you build your confidence in various areas as you move along in your self-development journey. You'll also have to put in tremendous effort in working on what you believe about yourself and how you love yourself to develop healthy self-esteem.

Below are some action steps you can take to help improve your self-confidence:

- Acknowledge the areas you'd like to improve or grow in and draw up an action plan for how to work on each one of them.
- Ask your close friends and family members what they think about your strengths and weaknesses and listen to their suggestions of what you can do to improve things. Being receptive to constructive feedback helps you to keep growing.
- Invest more time and effort in honing what you are good at; this will help you become more competent in your key talents and unique abilities.
- Try new things, especially the things you feel insecure about. The more you practice doing something you aren't good at, the better you will get at it. This also makes you good at more things, which will help you maintain your confidence.
- Continue looking for ways to improve how you do things. This will make you even better at what

you already do well, and it will help keep your confidence high.

Here are some things you can do to significantly improve your self-esteem:

- **Reframe negative limiting beliefs about your worth by regularly using affirmations that reinforce a positive self-identity.**

Your beliefs shape your outlook on yourself and others, so make it a goal to never compare yourself to others but to instead practice embracing and appreciating your uniqueness. It's so easy to fall into the trap of comparing ourselves with others. The pressure is even worse when you are a teen, which is why it's important to practice being grounded in your core values and living a life true to what you believe in.

- **Build a greater sense of security.**

We derive a sense of safety and belonging when we have solid relationships with people who are important to us. These people can help you remember your worth and value in times when you may be questioning these things. You can do this by strengthening your relationships with family and close friends. Letting people in can be hard, especially when you struggle to put your trust in others. However, what I have come to understand about human nature is that when we treat people well and show them that we trust them, they often rise to the occasion. By learning to trust and show faith in others, you will be able to find people who are worthy of your trust, and your relationships will blossom and grow. You may even find others to connect with who are looking for the same kind of friendships you are looking for—authentic and fulfilling. Through your genuine friendship, you may inspire others to be their best selves. It's like the teacher that all the students love because she is so kind and understanding; they may give other teachers a hard time, but because that one teacher shows them the respect and warmth they crave, they will always behave for her. You can earn that kind of respect from others when you choose to treat them well.

- **Try not to ruminate on your past mistakes or unkind words others may have said to or about you.**

It's usually our own negative self-talk that impedes the health of our self-esteem. When you focus on the mistakes you have made, judge yourself harshly, or draw false conclusions about yourself, it only affects your perception of how special you are. It's hard to love someone you perceive as being "wrong," "flawed," or "not good enough." Therefore, you can improve your self-esteem by forgiving yourself for mistakes you may have made and not allowing other people's opinions to determine how you view yourself. Whenever you catch yourself dwelling on negative messages or memories, you can stop those thoughts right away and distract yourself by watching your favorite show, reading a good book, listening to your favorite music, or doing something else that makes you feel good. You might also want to write in a gratitude journal where you can keep a record of all the things you are thankful for about yourself and your life. In moments when you are feeling down and questioning yourself, make it a habit to grab that journal, snuggle up somewhere cozy, and immerse yourself in all the beautiful things you know and believe about yourself. As human beings, we can be very forgetful, and that's a terrible habit because we can even end up forgetting how wonderful we are. Thankfully, through journaling or even making a nice video diary about your life, you can remind yourself of how special you are in times when your spirits are down.

- **Reparenting yourself is another way you can build your self-esteem.**

If you grew up in an unstable home where you were neglected or felt unworthy of love, chances are your self-esteem is low because of those childhood wounds. The bright side is that it's never too late to reverse all the negative messages you grew up believing. Now that you are a young adult, you are no longer in the helpless position of a child who is unable to meet their needs on their own.

You can now work on validating yourself internally instead of doing things to seek other people's approval.

- **Embrace your authentic self and let go of the different personas you put on to try to fit in.**

Putting on a facade may get others to like you, but deep down you'll know that it's not truly *you* these people are getting to know. By embracing who you are, you practice self-acceptance, and this makes you more comfortable with yourself, which will naturally attract friends.

- **Consider working with a healthcare professional to recover from serious mental health concerns that may result from adverse past experiences.**

Sometimes people face horrible childhood experiences that cause acute post-traumatic stress disorder, such as extreme abuse or neglect. Such experiences can alter the trajectory of how someone feels about themselves for a long time. Before those events, the person may have had healthy self-esteem, but afterward, they might have experienced a drastic change in how they perceive themself. In such cases, enlisting the help of a psychologist or licensed therapist can help the victim survive that trauma and minimize its effect on the rest of their life. Teens who don't get help after experiencing such difficult situations may end up battling depression or being vulnerable to unhealthy relationships due to having low self-esteem. Working with a healthcare professional has the added advantage of not having to go through all those difficult emotions alone. Just knowing that someone knows your story in full, doesn't judge you, and is there to walk with you through every step of your recovery journey will help you feel better much faster than you might have thought possible.

Practicing these strategies will help you develop lasting healthy self-esteem. In the next chapter, we'll take an even deeper look into various ways that you can grow your self-esteem.

2

THE BEAUTY WITHIN

CULTIVATING SELF-ESTEEM

You yourself, as much as anybody in the entire universe, deserve your love and affection.

— SHARON SALZBERG

In the previous chapter, we talked about the difference between self-esteem and self-confidence. In this chapter, we will take a deeper look at self-esteem and identify factors that influence the way you feel about yourself. You will also learn some action steps you can take to begin developing healthy self-esteem.

As I mentioned earlier, your self-esteem encompasses how you feel about your worth and what you believe about yourself, which can either make you love yourself or struggle with self-acceptance. Your self-esteem can be influenced by your environment, age, socioeconomic status, thinking patterns, belief system, genetics, health status, body aesthetics, and sometimes disability.

If someone grew up in an environment where material possessions were often equated to a person's worth, this could greatly impact their self-esteem. This can be particularly challenging for people who grew up in a low-income home as they may feel this fact determines some level of their worth. It's important to recognize that money and possessions do not make a person worth more or less than anyone else, and people's feelings of self-worth should never be based on their material possessions. When someone believes that how much money they have determines their worth, that person may battle with their self-esteem for a long time. Basing your self-worth on the amount of money your family has is a superficial way to go through life because money is fleeting, making it an unreliable foundation to hinge your self-worth on. If you allow these kinds of things to affect how you feel about yourself, your self-esteem may diminish if your family is ever not doing well financially because financial circumstances can change. Unfortunately, we live in a society that places a lot of value on how much money someone has and people's socioeconomic status. It's fundamental to create a value system for yourself when you are young that will keep you from feeling the need to chase after validation based on how much money you have.

For instance, you can develop a set of values that includes

- treating everyone equally and not discriminating against anyone, including yourself, based on how much money they have.
- believing that the amount of money someone has does not determine their worth.
- not judging yourself or others based on socioeconomic status.
- knowing people's worth comes from who they are as human beings and how they treat others.

Being levelheaded and making good choices with your money, both when finances are tight as well as when they're flourishing, will help protect your self-esteem from being affected by how much money you have. When you are a teen, it can be tempting to flaunt your money when things are going well for you and your family, and you may even have an ego boost if things are going particularly well. While this may seem normal, it's actually a sign of poor self-esteem; you don't want how good you feel about yourself to rely on how much or little money your family has. Instead, practice being content with whatever situation you may be in. Whether things at home are going well financially or not, try not to let that affect how you view yourself. Valuing yourself regardless of money or possessions is what will attract others to you. People tend to treat others the way they treat themselves, so if they sense that you are insecure about your family's money situation, they may begin to treat you in ways that reinforce those feelings. This is why it's important to reflect on what you believe about yourself, as this will affect how people perceive you.

When it comes to genetics, have you ever noticed that most people who come from the same family usually have similar belief patterns or behaviors? For instance, you might have noticed that if parents are good at math, their kids will also probably be good at math, or if a family loves playing football, chances are the children brought up in that family will grow up being good at football. This shows us how parents often pass down certain traits and qualities to their children. So don't be surprised if you notice that you have grown up to be shy if your parents tend to be shy. Although genetics do affect a child's personality, the great news is that through intentional habit formation, you can overcome any qualities you have that may impede your healthy self-esteem. Habits are formed by diligently repeating actions that reinforce the qualities you wish to have. In the upcoming chapters, we will elaborate on how you can successfully build habits that promote healthy self-esteem.

Now, let's talk about health. One of the major things teens experience during puberty is increased hormonal activity, which can cause skin problems like pimples, blackheads, scarring, changes in pigmentation, and frequent break-outs. This can be even more difficult when you feel like your peers notice any skin issues you may be having, especially if they make unkind comments about it. Sometimes, you might experience an illness of some kind, making you feel insecure about yourself. These health challenges can make it difficult to muster healthy self-esteem. However, by working on your self-perception, you can break free from allowing these things to determine your worth. Whether you are ill or not, whether your skin is clear or not, it's important first to practice loving and accepting yourself for who you are. When you embrace your current developmental stage, others will respect you and be less likely to criticize or bully you for your health challenges.

Sometimes your health might be great, but your feelings about your body make you feel insecure and self-conscious. Teens often compare how they look to others. If you are a late bloomer, you might start to feel insecure that you haven't developed a beard, deep voice, muscles, breasts, or hips yet. It's normal to feel this way, but it's important to realize that wherever you are in your physical development doesn't make you any less than you are. Or perhaps it was the opposite for you: Maybe you developed much faster compared to the majority of your peers, or you might be dealing with weight issues. Regardless, your physical appearance does not determine your value in any way.

I know it's hard, especially if other kids make comments that make you feel bad for just being who you are. But remember that you can face and conquer any challenge that comes your way. You have the power within you to confidently stand up for yourself and proudly embrace all the changes your body is undergoing. It all starts with you. As long as you maintain a positive view of yourself, the opinions of others won't have as great an effect on you. People tend to respect those who clearly like and respect themselves, and you can take advantage of this fact by focusing on loving yourself rather than trying to meet others' expectations. Often, it's impossible to meet others' expectations anyway because they may be unrealistic or ever-changing, and those expectations vary from person to person, so there's no way to meet them all and no point in trying. Therefore, it's better to focus on being who you want to be and nothing else. Truly understanding who you are and what really matters to you will protect you from being a people pleaser. People-pleasing also reinforces low self-esteem because it focuses more on others than on yourself and can cause you to continue putting up a facade instead of confidently embracing who you are and allowing yourself the freedom to evolve.

Having healthy self-esteem means you have a positive relationship with yourself, and it also means that you appreciate everyone else for their unique differences. When you have healthy self-esteem, you allow yourself the freedom of expression, and when it's time to assert your boundaries, you don't hold back. Self-acceptance and love are at the core of building healthy self-esteem.

On the other hand, when someone is struggling with low self-esteem, they tend to focus on their weaknesses and downplay their achievements, and they hesitate to take on challenges. They often avoid people or having social interactions as they can trigger a lot of anxiety and stress. Poor self-esteem is also characterized by difficulty with advocating for oneself. There is also a strong belief that others are better than you. It's hard for people with low self-esteem to accept constructive criticism gracefully. This is because instead of open-mindedly reflecting on what they are hearing and using it to grow and do better next time, their minds tend to negatively interpret what they are hearing and allow it to reinforce their adverse self-perception. Receiving criticism makes them feel attacked, and as a result, it becomes difficult for them to change or even get along with others because they feel like all anyone ever sees is the "bad" things about them. When you think negatively about others, they will notice, and this can cause them to view you negatively in return and act according to that view, meaning they may not be as kind or friendly as they might have otherwise been. That is why being positive about others can help prevent you from being bullied or feeling like no one likes you. People often treat us the way we think they will, so if you think someone is a bully or out to get you, this may discourage the person from being positive toward you and may even encourage them to act the way you're projecting onto them. This happens because they already feel judged by you, and thus, the space for building a positive relationship is blocked.

Another major problem we should touch on is having excessive self-esteem. While it's great to have healthy self-esteem, you want to be aware of keeping your self-esteem in check by not becoming egotistical or full of yourself. Excessive self-esteem might look like someone believing they're better than others, judging others negatively, believing they're always right, or thinking only certain kinds of people are good enough to be their friends. People with negatively excessive self-esteem also believe others should always do what they want, and they may even start to overtly or covertly retaliate against those who don't cooperate with them. They may have a tendency to do things for attention in order to show off rather than just genuinely being who they are. Excessive self-esteem is off-putting because people will often put others down or be overly focused on achieving perfection to the point that they undermine the efforts of others if they feel they're less than perfect. It also makes people overestimate their capabilities, which can lead to disappointment and even more negative feelings.

In your journey to embracing confidence, it's important to be introspective so you can make sure you aren't projecting excessive or low self-esteem. Poor self-esteem can cause people to live in fear or constantly be in survival mode. You don't want to live your teen years feeling this way. Thankfully, this chapter will continue unpacking ways you can put an end to low self-esteem and start developing lasting healthy self-esteem.

ISSUES THAT MANIFEST FROM HAVING LOW SELF-ESTEEM

You might have noticed that no matter where you go, whether you change schools or after-school activities, you still face issues related to low self-esteem. This is because, though you have physically changed locations, you have not changed your mindset. To put an end to the painful cycle of low self-esteem, you instead need to intentionally focus on changing your belief system and ways of thinking. By healing what's hurting within, you give yourself the chance to rewrite your negative experiences into something more positive.

Now let's have a look at some of the problems that can be caused by low self-esteem:

- **Self-loathing:**

Do you ever struggle to love who you are or feel that you're unlikable? These feelings are not only unpleasant, but they can also hinder your confidence and self-esteem. Poor self-esteem indicates that you often feel negatively about yourself, and it can be hard to love yourself if you feel that way. This is one reason that external successes don't necessarily equate to healthy self-esteem. The way we view ourselves internally has a lot to do with whether we proudly show who we are outwardly or whether we try to hide who we are in the background. Self-loathing can lead to other problems such as feeling jealous or unhappy about others' success or even sabotaging your relationships because you believe you aren't good enough. Some teens may even deal with mental health issues if they struggle to love and accept themselves. How you love yourself affects how you treat yourself. When you dislike who you are, you are more likely to treat yourself poorly, which can lead to even more self-loathing or other problems, like being bullied. Bullies often target those who demonstrate low self-esteem, so this is another good reason to take care of yourself and work on accepting and loving who you are. When your self-love and acceptance are obvious to the world, others will be more likely to treat you with the same respect and kindness. One way to work on loving yourself is by utilizing mindfulness techniques such as meditation or positive daily affirmations. Meditation will help you become more aware of your thoughts, and affirmations will help build your self-esteem. Beyond changing how you think and speak about yourself, you also have to start doing things that show that you love yourself. Imagine all the things you would do for someone you really care about. How would you show that person how much you care for them and how would you treat them on a daily basis to continue showing your love? It's easy for us to come up with lots of ideas for what we can do for those we love, but it's just as important to do those things for ourselves too. Loving ourselves is the best way to attract love and acceptance from others.

- **Always feeling dissatisfied and unhappy with your efforts:**

Do you ever find yourself being overly critical of the things you do or feel as if those things have no significance? The inner critical voice of someone battling with low self-esteem tends to be very loud. That negative voice can be further amplified when your peers say unkind things that you may take to heart. With such a loud voice bringing you down, it can be hard to overcome the self-doubt. You may downplay or criticize your efforts so much that even others may notice and begin to seem to agree, which you may take as further confirmation that the negative voice in your mind is actually right when really those people are only mirroring what you're putting out into the world. This can create a painful cycle of projecting and receiving this kind of energy. Thus, it's important to acknowledge and appreciate your efforts to avoid burning out or losing the motivation to keep trying. This ultimately highlights your failures instead of pushing you forward to achieve your goals. Do you have a hard time giving yourself credit when you deserve it? If so, try to start noticing your efforts and being your own cheerleader by celebrating every achievement—big and small—because you are indeed trying!

- **Constantly doubting yourself:**

Do self-doubt and indecision affect your confidence? Indecision is one of the biggest challenges people with low self-esteem face. People who struggle with low self-esteem tend to base their identity and feelings of worth on what others think about them, which makes it hard to have a solid identity and know what you really want. When that's the case, it is hard to feel confident in the decisions you make. Instead of checking in with yourself to see if a decision aligns with your values or goals, you might instead find yourself looking to others to give you answers. You might also not have a clear idea of what you want but are very aware of what others want from you. Instead of having faith in your dreams and goals, you end up doubting them and believing that what others think is best for you is what you should settle for. Self-doubt impedes confidence and gets in the way of you taking advantage of many opportunities that you can grow from. It makes choosing to stay in your comfort zone seem so much more appealing than taking any positive risks. Just as people find it difficult to like someone who doesn't like themself, self-doubt also makes others doubt you. Knowing yourself well and choosing to stand up for what you believe in despite facing any criticism helps you to be anchored and move past your self-doubt. We all experience some level of self-doubt almost daily, but what matters is learning how to not allow that doubt to dictate your decisions. Where you feel doubtful of yourself, choose to exercise faith instead, and you may be pleasantly surprised at how fortune favors the brave. The key is to simply take the action needed despite being unsure of your abilities. The only way to know if you can or cannot do something is to try, and the more you try and keep at something, the better you will become at it over time. So give yourself room for trial and error, and don't allow self-doubt or hesitation to stop you from going after whatever it is that you want.

• Feeling like the world isn't a safe place:

The world can indeed be an unsafe place, so it's important to do what you can to protect yourself in as many ways as possible. On the other hand, it's essential to recognize that there are safe places and that you can find a sense of security in this unpredictable world. Believing that you can't be safe anywhere or with anyone can hinder your ability to build lasting, meaningful relationships, and it's hard for others to be there for you unless you allow them to be.

• Often feeling down, anxious, or worthless:

Because of the internal turmoil that low self-esteem can cause in your mind and heart, you may find it hard to create lasting joy in your life. You may feel down no matter what you are doing, where you are, or who you're with. You may also feel distrustful when good things happen to you or come into your life or fearful that anything good you have may somehow be taken away from you someday. You may worry that close friends or even someone who shows a romantic interest in you may lose interest when they realize you struggle with low self-esteem. Thus, you end up trapped in a cycle of feeling like you don't deserve anything good happening to you, and when good things do happen, you may even end up sabotaging those things to avoid any kind of future rejection or pain. This is another example of experiencing imposter syndrome, which, if you remember from our discussion of it earlier, is when you feel like you aren't worthy of the success or happiness you're experiencing. This kind of self-perception can get in the way of you creating the life you want for yourself because every time you start to take steps to do so, you end up second-guessing yourself and giving up or settling for less. Feelings of worthlessness and anxiety then become familiar, especially in your relationships with others. Feeling this way can make it hard to sustain happy and healthy relationships because others can pick up on the way you feel about yourself, and that negative energy can make it difficult for relationships to thrive. It's hard to feel at ease or comfortable in your own skin when battling with low self-esteem, which is why those who deal with low self-esteem may feel awkward or uncomfortable, especially in social situations. If you often notice feelings of sadness, emptiness, or low self-worth, this may be a sign that you are experiencing low self-esteem.

- **Undermining the importance of your opinion:**

Have you ever had something valuable to contribute to a group conversation but couldn't bring yourself to speak up and share? Sometimes a lack of self-esteem can cause us to question ourselves and lead to us suppressing our voice to avoid speaking out, even when we really want to. You may become used to undermining your own opinion and being overly agreeable even when your contribution would have improved or helped whatever circumstance you were in. Furthering the difficulty of this is the feelings of sadness that may follow as you recognize that you are silencing yourself, which can lead to you feeling disappointed in yourself, perpetuating the cycle of low self-esteem. The problem with never speaking out is that people may start to view you in ways that are inaccurate or unfair, such as that you don't want to contribute or you don't have anything useful to share. Practice articulating your thoughts out loud when you're alone, maybe even in front of a mirror, so that you will be more used to it the next time you find yourself in this kind of situation. When you can voice your opinions and ideas clearly, people will begin to listen to and respect you, opening the door to new relationships and opportunities.

- **Being unable to self-advocate or be assertive:**

Being assertive is respectfully standing up for yourself and stating your ideas or point of view. This is also closely related to self-advocacy. When someone is struggling with low self-esteem, they tend to subconsciously believe they don't deserve the best or to be treated well. As a result, when others treat them poorly, they may not realize that how they are being treated is toxic or they might end up having a high tolerance for poor treatment. This can make them afraid or unable to speak up for themselves and say they don't want to be treated that way. If we can't express our concerns about how we are being treated, the other person will likely continue with the same behaviors. This either happens because we allow them to or because they aren't aware of how it's affecting us. Relationships, no matter what kind—family, friends, teachers, coaches, classmates, teammates, and so on—can only be strong if we communicate effectively and help others understand what our needs are. It can be very hard for someone dealing with low self-esteem to advocate for themselves, and they may struggle in their relationships due to a lack of effective communication. Usually, the fear of rejection or assuming that bottling our emotions protects other people's feelings from being hurt causes people to avoid being assertive and speaking their minds. Ironically, it's quite the opposite. If we don't speak our minds when we should, it hurts you and others because, in the long run, people are connecting to an inauthentic version of you instead of the real you. To solve this dilemma, it's always best to be honest with others about how you feel. If you need to have a conversation with someone about how they treat or talk to you, choose a good time and place free of distractions to share your thoughts and feelings respectfully but assertively. Be ready to listen, but more importantly, be prepared to stand up for yourself.

- **People-pleasing:**

This is a common coping mechanism people battling with low self-esteem tend to have. It's easy to convince ourselves that if we agree with others, do what they want us to do, or just "go with the flow," people will like us more. You may even find that people are nicer or more friendly after going out of your way to accommodate them, but this outcome can be short-lived. It sometimes only lasts for as long as that person is pleased with what you did, but as soon as they want something else from you, they may rescind their kindness until you accommodate them once again. Relationships founded on this dynamic seldom last because people-pleasing allows someone to take advantage of you. Instead, figure out who you really are and what will make you happy, and chase after that instead.

- **You are highly sensitive about what others think of you:**

Because those with low self-esteem tend to have a negative opinion of themselves and also tend to place a lot of value in what others think of them, it's easy to be hurt by others. You may be highly sensitive to what others think of you and constantly seek out their approval and validation. When you learn that someone has a less-than-favorable opinion of you, you may internalize that and believe it to be true rather than recognizing that others' opinions have more to do with them than with you. This can make you vulnerable to emotional and verbal abuse. However, if you want to reverse this and build healthier self-esteem, try to practice being grounded in what you think of yourself and caring less about what others think of you. Giving people that power over you can be harmful. Bullies who target others whom they view as weak may notice that anything they say can set the tone for your mood or day, and they may use that knowledge to hurt you. But if you show the rest of the world that you couldn't care less about other people's opinions, those kinds of people will move on from targeting you. Often, those kinds of bullies only continue their behavior as long as it appears to have an effect on their victim. You may notice that bullies rarely target those who appear confident and carefree. Do your best to internalize that confidence and freedom, and it will eventually become your reality as you project that energy into the world.

- **Struggling with anger or constant irritability:**

The constant stifling of self-expression leads to having many bottled-up feelings. This can make you prone to irregular mood swings and even emotional outbursts. If you feel like you are often on edge and irritated by people, you might need time to vent out what's been bothering you. Finding a confidant you can trust and talk to about what's on your mind is essential. This helps you verbalize what you are going through and get those negative feelings out in the open in a healthy way. Holding your feelings in can lead to outbursts or taking things out on those you care about, so expressing your emotions and talking about your experiences in a safe environment can also help improve your interpersonal relationships.

- **Poor performance and having a fixed mindset:**

As human beings, we are constantly evolving. If you have poor self-esteem now, it doesn't mean that you will have low self-esteem forever. You can choose to make changes and become someone completely different. However, people with low self-esteem tend to have difficulty believing that it's really possible for them to be free from their current way of processing reality. This fixed way of thinking can make it hard to take the necessary steps toward change. However, since you are here reading this book, I know that you have the motivation and power within you to take those steps and shift your mindset.

When your self-esteem is healthy, it positively impacts every area of your life. You begin to have an "I can do this" mentality, and that alone will set you up for success.

Now, let's look at some helpful action steps you can take to overcome low self-esteem and master healthy self-esteem for good.

ACTION STEPS TO BOOST SELF-ESTEEM

To help you remember what we have covered so far, here are some practical tips you can keep handy as you initiate changes that will help you build healthy self-esteem:

- Never allow other people's opinions of you to define you or determine how you feel about yourself.
- Be true to yourself. Those who deserve to be in your life will accept you for who you truly are, and those who aren't true to you might walk away when you are the real you, and that's okay.
- Practice speaking your mind, even if it scares you. The more you do this, the less afraid you will be to be assertive.
- Treat yourself well. People respect and love someone who loves and respects themself. You attract the same energy as you put out.
- Keep working on improving yourself without forgetting to appreciate how far you have come.

Celebrate who you are at every point of your journey.

- Have reasonable expectations for yourself. Set attainable goals and be honest about your skills and competence. This gives you the humility to ask for help when you need it. Asking for help doesn't mean you are weak, nor does it diminish your worth.

- Give yourself permission and space to make mistakes. Some of the greatest discoveries were made by people who were willing to take healthy risks. Everyone makes mistakes, and doing so doesn't make you any less worthy.

- Think and talk positively about yourself and shut down your negative inner critic by replacing negative thoughts with encouraging ones.

- Focus on validating yourself instead of chasing after external validation, and choose to no longer be a people pleaser.

- Challenge yourself to do things you have never done before—this helps awaken you to your limitless potential and appreciate yourself more.

- Establish healthy boundaries to protect every aspect of your life. Make it a point to always communicate them respectfully to others so that they understand how you expect to be treated.

As you read this list, you may have come up with more ideas for other great action steps you can take to boost your self-esteem. Make a note of all those ideas and journal your journey. Journaling will help you evaluate and review your progress, which, in turn, will give you greater insight into ways you can keep making the most of your efforts to master unwavering self-esteem. In the next chapter, we'll dive into the different strategies you can employ to rise above your insecurities.

3

RISING ABOVE INSECURITIES

> *To be beautiful means to be yourself. You don't need to be accepted by others. You need to accept yourself.*
>
> — THICH NHAT HANH

One of the biggest insecurities many teens face is their body image. In fact, this insecurity can last well into our adult years and even continue for the rest of our lives if left unremedied. Today's world is making it even harder for people to have genuine self-confidence and self-acceptance because of the unrealistic beauty ideals promoted in the media and online. Most teens spend much of their free time on social media and are bombarded by images of heavily filtered and airbrushed people looking their very best. Social media has many benefits, but teens must also be aware that not everything they see and hear on social media is reality.

First of all, just because someone isn't yet an adult filled with worries about bills and adult responsibilities doesn't mean that their life is any easier. Sadly, sometimes grown-ups seem to forget that being a teenager is also very challenging as you have to deal with so much in every aspect of your life. Teens are faced with pressures such as feeling like they have to fit in with a particular group of friends, not speaking up when they see others being bullied for fear of becoming the bully's next target, having to maintain good grades, trying to be good enough for your family and friends to accept you, trying to find yourself and make choices that won't jeopardize your future, and understanding your own body and the rapid changes it's undergoing. As if that's not enough, you still have to come home and do your part in helping with family errands and chores. All of this can be overwhelming for a teen who was a carefree child not too long ago.

Knowing how to deal with feeling insecure about your body can save you from many problems that can arise from having a poor body image. First, what exactly do we mean when we are talking about body image? Your body image is how you perceive your body, which, in turn, determines the relationship you have with your body. This means that someone can either have a positive or negative body image depending on what they think and believe about their body.

Many teens wonder what they can do to develop a healthy body image. It's important to understand that having a healthy body image does not mean you will never want to change something about your body. That would be a rather unrealistic expectation. We all have parts of ourselves we wish were somewhat different, and that's totally normal and a part of being human. In fact, believe it or not, even the most popular students in school have their share of insecurities, although they would never admit it. Having a truly positive body image means you accept and appreciate your body the way it is, including the parts you love and the parts you wish you could change. Self-acceptance is so important because it influences how you treat yourself, especially around others. If you are critical of your body and allow your negative inner voice to take over every time you look in the mirror, it may eventually damage your confidence. When you accept your body as it is, you acknowledge that there are parts of your body you love more than others without feeling ashamed of the parts you don't love. It also means that you are giving yourself room to work on what you want to change—if it's possible—and navigate through life still loving yourself fully.

This self-acceptance gives you the chance to positively experience life without facing challenges that having a poor self-image can put in your way. The benefits of having a positive and healthy body image are worth pursuing because it can save you from dealing with the extra stress and needless pressures many teens grapple with. For instance, when you have a healthy body image, you are more likely to make friends and go to social gatherings confidently, display positive body language, and have more time to invest in your studies and other meaningful things. On the other hand, teens who struggle with a poor body image tend to avoid social gatherings as these can make them feel very uncomfortable, and they may have a harder time making friends due to a lack of confidence. They might even get the unwanted attention of a bully, have trouble keeping up with their schoolwork, or lose interest in once-loved hobbies or activities because that negative perception of themselves slips into other aspects of their lives and holds them back from completely embracing their full potential.

The great news is that no matter how negative your perception of your body may be, you can radically change that by learning to quiet your loud inner critic and replace that vicious voice with a healthier, more encouraging voice. This is the voice that will remind you that you are beautiful and your worth is not determined by parts of your body but instead by what you have to contribute to the world. It becomes your own personal cheerleader rather than fueling the negative self-talk in your head. By mindfully practicing self-acceptance, you will come to understand that your self-love shouldn't be limited to only the parts of yourself that you assume society approves of—true self-love and confidence come from being able to appreciate all of who you are with genuine compassion and kindness. It is people who confidently show who they really are—especially the parts of themselves that they might not fully embrace—that end up having the healthiest body images. It all starts with learning to proudly show who you are with an attitude that declares, "This is my true identity, and I am proud of myself!" Really and truly, when you finally awaken to the reality that people who have the best experiences in life are the people who have learned to love all of who they are, you will no longer allow yourself to be disappointed by any part of who *you* are. As you begin to love and appreciate yourself more authentically, others will become more and more attracted to you. That's how it works! We perceive the things people are proud of as being desirable and beautiful. Therefore, when you start unashamedly embracing everything that makes you who you are and changing the way you carry yourself so that your pride in yourself is evident to all, you become more attractive and feel more confident.

At this point, you might be unsure whether you have a poor or healthy body image. To help you determine that, in the next section, we'll look at some points that will help you identify the subtle and overt signs of people who battle with negative body image.

COMMON SIGNS OF TEEN BODY IMAGE INSECURITIES

Sometimes it can be hard to understand how you feel about your body. Some days you may feel totally in love with your body, and other days can be more difficult, especially if you are unhappy with what you see in the mirror for one reason or another. You may shy away from looking in the mirror at all because of this, but you will still feel that discontent with your body. Your inner critic may take over and begin its expert duty of loudly pointing out all your perceived flaws, reinforcing your low self-confidence, and bringing you down. It's important to reflect on your relationship with your body because it is hard to find genuine love from others when we can't even genuinely love ourselves. On the other hand, the more positive your relationship with your body is, the more likely others are to accept you as you are. Now let's explore some common signs of someone who is struggling with a poor body image.

- **Frequently checking the mirror to confirm that you look okay:**

It's okay to enjoy looking at yourself in the mirror. In fact, it's not a bad idea to check how you look before leaving the house each day. However, the problem comes when you obsessively check the mirror because you feel insecure about your appearance. If you are too self-conscious and get trapped in the habit of trying to make everything "just right," it robs you of the freedom to be yourself without feeling like you are being forced to meet unrealistic ideals. Usually, the most self-assured people carry themselves confidently whether they are sporting lounge clothes and a hat or messy bun or are dressed to the nines without a hair out of place. You can get there by intentionally practicing acting confident on days when you feel like your hair or outfit isn't on point because your confidence should not only be limited to times when you spend hours getting yourself ready. Don't worry if other people notice that your hair is messy or your clothes are wrinkly —in the long run, it doesn't really matter, and neither do their opinions. However you look, practice being confident in the body you have, and in doing so, you will show that your confidence is not determined by external attributes but is instead rooted in how much you believe in your unchanging self-worth.

- **Apologizing too much:**

Some teens who struggle with feeling confident may often feel the need to apologize for some aspect of themselves. This should never be the case. Expect people to accept you as you are and for who you are. Your body is wonderful and capable, and there is certainly nothing for you to apologize for. Sometimes, feeling insecure about your body can make you want to hide parts of yourself that you don't feel good about, but doing this only reinforces the idea that something is actually wrong with you or your body. I had a friend once who sustained major burns on her chest. The scars were very noticeable, and many people assumed she'd be self-conscious about them when they initially met her. Much to their surprise, she was not bothered at all—it was like she didn't even notice them. She would confidently wear tops that revealed the burn marks, and she did so in such an innocent way. You could tell that she never allowed that burn to make her feel insecure about herself. Her confidence was still flourishing, and many people were envious of her confidence. Because of the attitude and mindset she had about her body, everyone else started to perceive the situation through her eyes. You could tell that the burn became completely insignificant, and no one seemed to worry or be bothered by it at all. People treated her with the utmost respect because of the way she respected and loved herself. This taught me an incredible lesson about the importance of embracing all of you, no matter what the situation might be. Don't hide it—the more you love, accept, and freely embrace your body exactly as it is, the less power it will have in eroding your confidence.

• **Body-bashing yourself:**

This is an unhealthy habit many teens and even adults tend to resort to as a defense mechanism. People might make self-deprecating jokes or negative comments about their bodies to show others that they see their own imperfections; it's like they're trying to make fun of themselves before someone else can. This is wrong. The more you say negative things about your body, the more that narrative becomes ingrained in your mind. Your words have the power to shape your reality. Avoid speaking words that demean who you are, such as "Oh gosh, I hate my legs" or "I don't like my hair." These are simple examples of some of the negative things someone might say about themself that can easily become normalized. What you tell yourself over and over becomes what you believe, and what you believe affects your reality and perception, so tell yourself how special and beautiful/handsome you are every day and allow this to become your true belief and eventual reality in order to develop greater confidence in your body.

- **Avoiding social gatherings:**

Social gatherings can be nerve-wracking if you are self-conscious about your body. You might worry that people will be judging or making fun of you while you are there. A simple nonchalant glance may have you concluding that everyone there is laughing at you. If you tend to decline invitations to social events or gatherings, you may want to reflect on why that may be. Recognizing and seeking to understand our behaviors and why we engage in them can help us address the root cause of the problem. Chances are that if you avoid being around others, you have probably created a narrative about everything that could go wrong in any social situation. But take a moment to realize that this is something you've made up in your own mind and is unlikely to be what will actually unfold. However, if you choose to change the story and believe the best, you might be surprised at how great of an adventure you can have. Ask yourself what negative fictional stories you have been believing about your body and what would happen if you put yourself out there. After you see how unrealistic and harmful those stories are, take some time to write down a story or two about how great your life could be if only you embraced yourself as you are and confidently socialized with others. The more you think about and visualize those positive scenarios, the more likely you are to start believing them and gradually replicating them.

- **Displaying low-confidence body language:**

Body language is one way to determine whether someone feels confident in their own skin. For instance, people who struggle with confidence and body image may slouch a lot or try to take up as little room as possible, as if they are trying not to be noticed. Girls who feel self-conscious about their developing breasts or breast size may try to hide their bodies by changing their posture, and some teens may use baggy or oversized clothing to camouflage their bodies. In order to counteract this, practice using confident body language such as taking longer strides, holding your head high and shoulders back, making good eye contact, and using open gestures.

- **Obsessively checking your weight and having unhealthy eating habits:**

It's okay to check your weight here and there, but if you are constantly on the scale, that might be a telltale sign of a poor body image. Another dangerous behavior is when teens start to binge eat and then self-induce vomiting so that they won't gain weight. Starving yourself or eating too many unhealthy foods can indicate a problem with how someone views their body. Those who struggle with eating disorders do so because of their insecurities about their bodies. They often share a common denominator: the belief that people are always looking at their bodies and judging them. The truth is that, yes, sometimes people do judge others based on how they look. However, this only has power over you if you allow it to. If someone seems intent on making you feel bad about your body, try to demonstrate that others' opinions don't mean anything to you, and they will eventually turn their focus else-where. As long as you continue to love your body just the way it is, the external criticism is bound to diminish. If someone persists in antagonizing you, remember that this has nothing to do with you and that the person likely has their own issues they need to work on instead. Most people don't really spend a whole lot of time thinking about how others look—in fact, most teens are just as preoccupied with their own bodies as you are! Thus, the belief that people are always judging you is certainly not always the reality, and it's usually all in your head. Once you realize that, you will find the freedom to openly embrace your body without being self-conscious.

• **Comparing yourself to other people:**

You may feel that if only your body looked like this person's or that person's, then you'd finally be confident, but in fact, comparing yourself to others only brings down your self-esteem. It's important to focus on appreciating your body as it is and to understand that we're all made differently, and there's no one in the world who is exactly like you—and that's a good thing! If you often find yourself wishing you looked like someone else, this is a sign that your relationship with your body needs to be mended. One way to do this is to start a friendly competition... with yourself. This allows you to love yourself while working on improving the things you'd like to change. You get to forget about unrealistic body and appearance standards and focus instead on getting more exercise and eating a healthy, well-balanced diet so that you can help your body develop to its fullest ability.

- **Feeling as if you're not good enough to be friends with certain people:**

You may have noticed at your school or in other social situations that some kids tend to hang out with kids who are just like them and don't seem to branch out much, maybe even to the point that they purposely exclude those who are "different." This kind of cliquey behavior can be hurtful if you're not part of the "popular" group, and it may even begin to affect your self-esteem. This may lead to you feeling like you aren't deserving of healthy relationships with worthwhile people, and you may end up settling for less-than-healthy relationships as a result. Someone who finds themselves in this situation may start to isolate themself from others and become detached from former interests or hobbies because they feel like a misfit. If this has been your experience, I deeply understand how painful it can be. You can overcome these challenges by learning to base your value on your inner worth and who you are deep down rather than appearances. You are more than your body. Try to exercise bravery and dare to dream bigger, no longer settling for less but working hard to achieve the kind of interpersonal relationships you long to have.

LOVING YOUR BODY AND BUILDING A POSITIVE BODY IMAGE

Your body image influences a major part of your confidence, so it's important that you practice habits that will help you reinforce a positive body image every day. We have already extensively discussed ways to identify and stop having a poor body image. To ensure that you have a comprehensive list of action steps you can take to build a positive body image and love your body more than ever, let's review these tips:

- Interrupt negative self-talk and replace it with positive statements about how amazing your body is and how much you love it.
- Accept your body as it is by celebrating the things you love about it and accepting the parts you like the least without shame. Give yourself room to grow—your body is constantly changing, and how you look now is not how you will always look.
- Change your mirror talk. Look at yourself with compassion and acceptance. Hype yourself up whenever you are in front of the mirror and appreciate your beauty.
- Work on developing confident body language.
- Let go of all the limiting beliefs you have about your body.
- Practice being confident at all times, not only when you think you look your best.

- Eat healthily and work out regularly. Exercise and good food help to enhance your beauty naturally.
- Explore fashion styles that best complement your body type.
- Quit measuring yourself by unrealistic social media beauty standards.
- Maintain a positive perception of your body and always radiate a positive attitude about it, even when you don't feel like it. Our feelings can change if we are consistent in the actions we take.
- Loving your body doesn't mean you will always feel great about every part of it; instead, it is choosing to show your entire body love and appreciation even if you don't feel like it.

THE HEALING POWER OF MIRROR WORK

Of all the relationships you will ever have, one relationship you need to intentionally nurture is your relationship with yourself. The way you treat yourself sets the tone for how you will allow others to treat you, so if you ever feel dissatisfied in your interpersonal relationships, the first place to look to for improvement is your relationship with yourself. People are naturally drawn to people who accept and love themselves, which is why pleasing people doesn't really help you build genuine connections. Pleasing others while suppressing your true self shows that you don't respect and love yourself enough, which, in turn, may cause others to take advantage of you. We all go through phases where we struggle to love ourselves, but it's important to recognize when you're feeling that way and take steps to help bring positivity back into your life. Each day, you have the opportunity to build a better relationship with yourself, and by investing in various forms of self-care, you can strengthen that relationship at every opportunity.

Mirror work is a powerful healing tool that can help silence the negative self-talk that may pop up all too often in your mind. It is a technique that can help you reprogram your mind and change the way you feel and think about yourself. Many people feel a flood of negative thoughts or even a sense of shame when they look in the mirror because they are battling to accept how they look and who they are. These uncomfortable feelings can cause you to avoid looking at yourself in the mirror or shy away from having your photo taken because you don't like looking at your own image. Reality is composed of the perception people have about the world and themselves. This means that if you have an unhealthy self-image, your reality will likely be difficult, and you will find it hard to believe that you are beautiful and to love yourself the way you deserve. Thankfully, there is a way to shift that perception and change how you view and think about yourself for good. You will begin to see your beauty and true worth as the negative lenses you used to view yourself through fade away. This new perception of yourself can be deepened and solidified the more you continue to replace negative beliefs and thoughts you have about yourself with positive beliefs and thoughts that are more empowering and uplifting.

Just as any relationship will flourish with great communication, compassion, and love, your relationship with yourself can only change for the better when you start to intentionally cultivate seeds of love, good communication, compassion, and acceptance. Sometimes the idea of self-care sounds expensive, but thankfully, you don't need to worry about spending funds on anything with this technique—all you need is a mirror and a few minutes of your time each day.

Negative thoughts can get more insistent after something bad happens, such as losing a competition you were participating in or if someone says something mean to you. It is especially during those times of emotional turbulence and pain that you have to counter the flood of negative thoughts swirling in your mind and take control by choosing to do mirror work. Using positive affirmations when you are feeling hurt or in doubt about your worth helps you avoid further emotional damage from happening the next time something bad transpires. Aside from using mirror work to soothe and help your mind focus on the positive during a difficult time, you can also regularly practice this technique as part of your daily self-care routine. Think of it this way: Every time you sow love for yourself during your mirror work exercises, it's like someone watering a delicate flower—

providing what it needs to thrive. Similarly, the way you feel about yourself is bound to drastically change the more you consistently nurture yourself in this meaningful way.

To start incorporating mirror work into your life, let's take a look at some steps you can follow:

1. Sit or stand comfortably in front of your mirror, and make sure you can see your whole face and body.
2. Take deep breaths as you gather your thoughts and focus solely on the present moment.
3. Gaze at your reflection with love and compassion —no judgment at all. Just take yourself in as you intently observe all of who you are. Start appreciating every body part and notice it for what it is.
4. If there are any emotions you're dealing with, let them out and genuinely express your love and appreciation for yourself. Use this time to clear out any negative thoughts by replacing them with positive self-affirmations, such as "My mistakes do not define me, and it's okay to make mistakes because that proves that I am learning and moving forward." If you are battling with accepting your body you can say, "I'm so sorry for taking so long to see and appreciate this exquisite beauty I now see—I love my body, and I am

beautiful/handsome and special in my own unique way."

5. Continue to repeat the affirmations out loud until you feel the power of each word you are saying in your heart. Smile and gaze at your reflection with genuine appreciation.

6. If there is anything you want to work on improving about your body, start visualizing your desired outcome now. For instance, you can say, "I am going to work out at least three times a week this month—I'm super excited!" This positive attitude shows that you are accepting of who you are but also open to working on yourself from a place of loving your body rather than feeling ashamed of it.

7. As you bring your mirror work session to a close, say "I love you" to your reflection. Love breathes life into our souls, and that includes your soul too! The more you express your love for yourself, the more appreciative you will be of all of who you are.

And that brings us to the end of the exercise! As you continue to practice this technique, you can edit your affirmations and make them resonate with any goal you want to achieve or any challenge you are facing. Writing your affirmations down gives you room to be who *you* want to be. I highly recommend writing them on sticky notes and putting them directly on your mirror or wall.

Sometimes we can drown in other people's expectations of who they think we should be, but being more aware of what you want for yourself helps your voice to not be overridden by the other voices all around you. The mirror exercise is time-tested and has helped many people heal their wounded inner child and become the best versions of themselves. Guess what? Now it's your turn!

Take some time to write a self-compassion letter to your body. You can use this letter to apologize to yourself for all the times you didn't take care of your body, talked badly about it, and felt ashamed of it. Use your gratitude journal to write about your journey toward learning to fully love and accept your body. The more you decide to love your body and no longer ruminate on negative beliefs and thoughts about it, the stronger and more confident your body image will be. Don't give up on working to improve your self-image and increase your self-love, even if it gets hard, because the outcome will be so worth it. Now let's take another important step and learn how you can effectively deal with bullies in your life. The next chapter will help you understand why people bully others and how you can strategically overcome bullies with confidence.

SPREADING THE CONFIDENCE

"Self-confidence can be learned, practiced, and mastered – just like any other skill. Once you master it, everything in your life will change for the better."

— BARRIE DAVENPORT

You're soaking up a ton of information here, so let's take a breather for a moment and reflect on how far you've come. You picked up this book because you were determined to build your confidence, and that was a huge step in itself. Now you're collecting strategies and beginning to believe in the incredible person you are, no matter what challenges you've faced that have brought you to this moment.

As you're hopefully seeing as we move through the book, there are plenty of things you can do to improve how you feel about yourself step by step… and as you start working on it, you'll begin to notice a change. You'll notice the opportunities around you, and you'll be less scared of exploring them; you'll overcome setbacks more quickly; you'll become more interested in looking outside of your comfort zone.

Perhaps you'll also notice more often when other people are struggling with their confidence – and as you do, you'll start to see that this issue affects far more young people than you might have realized.

I want to give as many teenagers as I can the tools they need to empower themselves and fight back against low self-esteem. I saw the difference in my son, and I know it's possible for everyone. So this is where I'd like to ask for your help in reaching more people, but don't worry – I don't need you to do anything more than write a few words.

By leaving a review of this book on Amazon, you'll show other teenagers who are struggling with their confidence exactly where they can find the help they're looking for.

It really is that easy. They're searching for this information, and it's reviews like yours that will help them find it.

Thank you so much for your support. Your voice matters.

Scan the QR code below to leave your review on Amazon.

4

THE BULLY BUSTERS

CONQUERING BULLYING WITH CONFIDENCE

Never be bullied into silence. Never allow yourself to be a victim. Accept no one's definition of your life; define yourself.

— ROBERT FROST

Every teen deserves the space and freedom to be who they truly are without being made to feel bad about it. Bullying is a serious problem that many teens have faced, and it can keep victims from feeling safe around others while being true to themselves. Bullying is when someone uses words and actions to deliberately hurt someone else and make them feel powerless, intimidated, and threatened. Bullies tend to target people whom they perceive to be weak—someone they believe won't be able to stand up to them. This is what makes them feel emboldened enough to continue tormenting their victim.

They feel powerful when they get away with their hurtful actions without facing any consequences. They like seeing the impact their behavior has on their victim as it gives them a sense of superiority and control. Bullies may also target people who are different from them when it comes to things like appearance, interests, and family or cultural background. There may be a variety of reasons a bully chooses to engage in their behavior, and often, one of the main reasons bullies attack their victims is because of their own unresolved insecurities.

A bully may choose their target out of jealousy; if they struggle to do well in school or make friends, they may victimize someone who seems to achieve these things easily. Instead of working on themselves to improve their grades or get the friends and attention they want positively, bullies choose to engage in negative and harmful behaviors to alleviate their insecurities. This is when we see them stepping on other people to get ahead or trying to dim someone else's light by making them feel bad about themselves, which brings them down to the bully's level. Once the bully sees that they have caused pain to their victim, they start to feel better about themself because seeing someone else at their lowest gives the bully a false and toxic sense of control and power. It's important to note that bullying is completely unacceptable, and no matter why someone chooses to bully another person, it is not okay and should not be tolerated. Bullying is *never* the victim's fault. When you are young, it can be overwhelming and difficult to stand up to and overcome bullying. But don't worry, this chapter will provide you with powerful strategies to finally put an end to the cycle of bullying in your life.

Sometimes, teens may struggle to open up about how they are being bullied at school, at home, or in their social circle. This is often because the bully might threaten to treat the victim even worse if they dare to report them. So if you find yourself in a situation like this and feel bad about not being able to report your experience of being bullied to someone, please don't blame yourself because your fears are valid and reasonable. You might have already experienced things worsening if you tried to stand up for yourself. If the outcome caused you to no longer feel safe about attempting to protect yourself, that is totally understandable. It can be overwhelming and difficult when family and friends don't understand your situation. Perhaps you even tried to confide in someone and reach out for help, and no action was taken; you may have felt that reporting what's happening to you gets you nowhere and that no one is willing to help, leading to frustration and despair. I want you to understand that your feelings are valid, and you deserve to feel safe and supported.

Bullying is, unfortunately, a common occurrence regardless of where you live or go to school. It's heartbreaking when young people struggle with their self-esteem and identity because they have been subjected to bullying. I want you to know that I deeply understand how difficult it is to be relentlessly bullied when all you're doing is striving to live a peaceful, happy life. Thankfully, many victims of bullying have found a way to overcome their experiences, and it is possible for you to do so as well. You have the inner strength and are worthy of being happy and living the life you want to live. Once you understand the psychology behind bullying, you will be able to respond to it more effectively and objectively, allowing you to reclaim your power and take charge of your life. Bullies are only as strong as we believe them to be, and once you realize that most of what bullies do comes from a place of weakness and insecurity, you can empower yourself to rise above their treatment of you and remove the power you never meant to give them. You may even start to see that the bully is crying out for love and acceptance behind the facade of being tough and intimidating others just to feel powerful.

It's important not to blame yourself for being bullied because it is absolutely not your fault. It's helpful to recognize that people only throw stones at a tree bearing fruit, which means that bullies tend to attack someone they feel intimidated by or jealous of. It can be helpful to try to understand what it is about you that makes them so afraid of you and then instead of hiding your light like they want you to, find ways to courageously shine it even more brightly! By doing this, you show the bully that you refuse to change yourself to make them feel better and that you are in fact brave enough to be yourself no matter what others say or think about you. Toward the end of this chapter, we will go through some action steps that you can take to put an end to bullying and fearlessly step into your light. In this upcoming section, though, let's talk about the different types of bullying that exist so that you can identify clearly what is happening and how to respond appropriately to each type of bullying. This knowledge will help you recognize and counteract the toxic behaviors of bullies.

DIFFERENT TYPES OF BULLYING EXPERIENCED BY TEENS

Teens experience various forms of bullying, and each one is hurtful and can greatly damage someone's self-esteem and feelings of self-worth. Bullying is when someone chooses to deliberately hurt you as opposed to when someone unknowingly behaves in a way that affects you negatively. In this section, we'll look at the most common types of bullying.

Verbal Bullying

This is when someone uses words to hurt you. Sometimes the words themselves might not be hurtful, but the tone may be demeaning. For instance, if someone says something sarcastically with a smile that seems harmless but deep down has undertones of putting down the other person—that is classified as verbal bullying. Thus, verbal bullying is not only saying hurtful words but also relates to how it is being said and the energy of the intentions behind what is said. Verbal bullying can look and sound like the bully threatening, yelling, speaking disrespectfully, or insulting the victim. Bullies usually verbally bully others by making cruel and often untrue or irrelevant comments about their appearance, religion, sexual preferences, family background, mannerisms, dressing style, the way they speak, their competence in certain areas, or a disability.

Gaslighting is another common type of verbal bullying. Gaslighting is when someone makes you doubt your perception of an event or situation or even your own thoughts or tries to project their issues onto you. For example, someone who is insecure about their friendships or peer relationships may say something like "You're such a loser, no wonder no one likes you." After a while, you may start believing this negative narrative about yourself even if you have close genuine friends. This is an example of the bullying tactic we talked about earlier where the bully attempts to make their victim feel bad because they feel bad. The things a bully says when gaslighting their target are not true, so it's important to have a strong sense of yourself and awareness of the various things bullies will do to make others feel bad about themselves.

Relational Bullying

This type of bullying is often seen in middle and high school, and it's when a group of people refuse to socialize or even interact with people outside their clique. In this type of bullying, the bully group will intentionally exclude and ostracize their victim or victims by making it clear that they are not welcome or wanted within the group. There is often a ringleader or person who seems to be the driving force behind the behaviors. Sometimes the other group members might even individually disapprove of what the group is doing by bullying and excluding others, but they seldom ever speak up against it for fear of becoming the next target.

Relational bullying can be particularly harmful because once a "popular" group of kids starts to exclude and avoid an individual or other group of kids, it can trigger a pattern of others treating the victims in the same way. If a well-liked group rejects someone, it can influence other people to also avoid socializing with them. This can make the victim feel completely isolated. If you are experiencing this kind of bullying, you may begin to feel lonely even when you're surrounded by many people. You might even feel like everyone is against you, and this can cause you to lose confidence in yourself as you start to believe that you aren't worthy of love and acceptance. Relational bullies are experts at making others feel invisible. If you try to share your contribution in a group discussion, relational bullies might deliberately ignore you or be critical of what you say. Relational bullying can cause teens to want to avoid going to school or other social gatherings so they won't have to endure being ignored and left out. Though this may temporarily relieve the victim from being subjected to the mistreatment, it won't solve the problem permanently. Self-acceptance and showing others that you love yourself and won't allow their opinion or treatment of you to dictate the course of your life can help you rise above this type of bullying and even end the cycle. Relational bullies continue their behavior when they see that what they are doing is affecting their victim. However, if you focus on your life and learn to emotionally detach yourself from their tactics, you can minimize their influence on you. When you give off energy that shows people that you aren't afraid of rejection and that you love and accept yourself, it can greatly influence people to stop rejecting you. Remember that principle—people love and respect someone who loves and respects themself.

Physical Bullying

This is a deplorable type of bullying where the bully uses physical contact to hurt the victim. It can include behaviors such as hitting, pushing, kicking, forcefully touching you inappropriately, or physically preventing you from getting past them. Things such as hair-pulling, knocking things out of someone's hands, or kicking or pulling someone's chair out from under them are also considered physical bullying. When bullies believe they can intimidate others physically, they will use this to frighten or have control over others, but physical assault is a major offense that can get someone arrested. If you are experiencing physical bullying, it's best to report the matter to responsible adults such as your parents, school administrators or teachers, or the police. Physical bullying can also take place at home if a member of your family physically assaults you. It can also occur in romantic relationships when either one of the partners physically harms their significant other. Sometimes teens will silently endure this kind of treatment because they believe that the person hurting them loves them, but true love does not ever involve physical harm. If you are experiencing this in any of your family or romantic relationships, seek the help of a trusted adult right away and know that you deserve so much better.

Cyberbullying

This type of bullying has become more common as the internet has become a daily way of life for almost everyone. Cyberbullying is when someone communicates abusive or rude comments through social media, text, email, or in any digital way. This kind of bullying is something many people face for as long as they have an online presence. People will always have opinions about what others do and post online, but it's important not to take to heart what people say online because it's so easy to say nasty things and hide behind a screen. People generally find cyberbullying less easy to control compared to other types of bullying. Thankfully, with the advancement of technology, it's now possible to restrict someone from viewing or posting on your account or contacting you. The best way to avoid virtual bullies is to block and ignore them. Using more regulated platforms that allow you to control your account and enable privacy settings can also help. However, even after putting all these protective measures in place, it's important to still practice valuing your opinion above what others say because the more exposure you have to the world, the more critics you might come across, but don't let this stop you from moving forward. Think about some of the things you've seen people comment on some celebrities' posts and pages —some things are downright hurtful, but many celebrities are still thriving in their careers as they try to focus on the positive side of things. Even if people say negative things about you online, you have the power to invalidate virtual bullies by simply ignoring them or blocking their access to your account. If the bully is someone you know from school, you can also print their messages and use that as evidence when you report them to school administrators. This will allow for disciplinary actions to be taken that may hopefully help the bullies change their ways.

Now that we have explored the different kinds of bullying that commonly occur in our society today, let's discuss some useful strategies you can implement to counteract any bullying in your life or the lives of your loved ones.

POWERFUL ACTION STRATEGIES TO OVERCOME BULLYING

In this section, we'll talk about things you can do to prevent or respond to any bullying you may find yourself dealing with. You have the ability and power to stand up for yourself and make use of any of these strategies. You may feel nervous if you're not used to speaking out against bullying, but as you practice more and more, you will become more comfortable standing up to bullies and taking control of your life. Let's now dive into the action steps:

- **Set and maintain boundaries:**

Boundaries are the framework we use to decide how we expect and will allow other people to treat us. Without boundaries, people may intentionally or unintentionally do things that hurt or offend you, so boundaries can help protect you from being taken advantage of by others. They can also help you ensure you don't give more of yourself than you should in your friendships and other relationships. People will only know how we want them to treat us if we communicate our needs clearly and respectfully. This means that setting healthy boundaries around your time, personal space, emotional well-being, relationships, finances or any resources you have is appropriate and necessary to keep you feeling comfortable and safe. Take some time to define your boundaries, and maybe even write them down so you can look at them occasionally and make any changes you feel are needed. Once you've done this, be intentional about communicating your boundaries to others and holding firm to them as time goes on. You can also share with others the outcomes of crossing your boundaries, such as going low- or no-contact, so they are aware of what will happen if they do so. Be sure to be clear and consistent with your boundaries so others continue to respect them.

Examples of how you can set healthy boundaries include saying things like "I don't want to gossip about someone. Let's talk about something else." "When you need to use my personal things, please don't forget to ask." If someone touches you inappropriately, you can say something like "Please stop. I feel that's a very inappropriate and disrespectful way to touch someone. Please respect my personal space." If someone is emotionally abusing you with hurtful words, you can say something like "I'm not sure if you are aware of the impact of your words. They come across as very hurtful. Please change the way you speak to me and be mindful of what you say." As you assert yourself, it's very important that your tone and demeanor reflect how serious you are about what you are saying. This helps the other person understand the gravity of the matter and be less likely to repeat any offensive behaviors again.

- **Practice being true to yourself and avoid people-pleasing tendencies:**

Sometimes teens fall into the trap of trying to please bullies in the hope that this will get them on their good side. Unfortunately, this is an unhealthy coping mechanism that can set you up for being used and taken advantage of by others, and it does not allow for genuine relationships to develop because you are acting inauthentically. Being true to yourself and not worrying about what others think of you will ultimately gain your peers' respect because you are demonstrating that your self-worth comes from within. Bullying usually stops when you assertively stand up for yourself and show the bully that you won't let them have power in your life.

- **Practice self-acceptance and being okay with vulnerability:**

Many celebrities were bullied while growing up and even to this day still face a lot of cyberbullying. What's special about them is that even though they have been through their own share of rough patches and still deal with toxic people, they don't give those people the power to stop them from continuing to do well in their lives. Think about Selena Gomez, Justin Timberlake, Demi Lovato, and Rhianna, just to name a few; all of these icons faced extreme bullying, but they weren't afraid to share their stories openly and show the world how, despite those challenges, they were able to rise above them and become very successful (Yagoda, 2022). When they shared their stories about how they overcame bullying even from certain family members, the world loved them even more and their fan bases grew. Similarly, it's important to remember that there is no shame in revealing your scars to the relevant audience. It is by doing so that you can continue to grow and inspire others to support you and overcome their own challenging situations.

- **Respectfully but firmly ask the bully to stop:**

One of the most effective ways to end bullying is to directly face the bully and call them out on their inappropriate behavior, especially in front of others. Doing it privately can work, but it's even more effective to show them that you are brave enough to stand up for yourself in the public eye. When you call them out and show them how their behavior hurts others, make sure you do so respectfully but assertively so you don't stoop to their level of addressing others in deliberately hurtful ways. Objectively point out what they did that was wrong and explain why. Keep the conversation short and straight to the point. If you talk too much, you might come across as defensive, which doesn't always have the desired impact. Lengthy confrontations might also give the bully time to avoid the conversation or turn things around to make it sound like you are the problem. Make sure that your voice is clear and that you are loud enough but composed so that you come across as confident and sure of yourself—even if you don't feel that way in the moment. You might feel very nervous when standing up to a bully, and that's totally okay. You can help keep yourself calm by controlling your breathing with slow, deliberate breaths, as this can help you maintain composure and avoid shaking or showing obvious signs of nervousness.

- **Report bullying:**

Reporting bullying to teachers, guidance counselors, school administrators or resource officers, parents, or other trusted adults as early as possible helps to protect you from insistent bullies who thrive in their victim's silence. Bullies may try to threaten you into believing that not reporting them is for your own good, but in reality, there is always someone willing to help. If you've tried reporting being bullied before, but no one took any action, don't let that discourage you. Continue to actively seek someone you can confide in until you find a true listening ear and someone willing to take steps to help the situation. Chances are that before you can even tell five people, you will have already found someone willing to help you resolve the situation.

- **Try to ignore bullies and walk away:**

Bullies love attention. Whether it's positive or negative attention, as long as you are spending your energy on them, they're getting what they want. Walking away from a volatile situation or just ignoring them and acting unbothered by their attempts to bully you makes their quest to bring you down unsuccessful and therefore unsatisfying for them. It can be hard to rise above being bullied, but remember you have the inner strength to stand up for yourself and what you know is right.

- **Maintain composure and practice emotional regulation around them:**

Bullies are very good at picking up on nervous body language cues. To keep the bullies moving along, be aware of your body language: walk with a confident, upright posture, keep your chin up, and make natural eye contact. This shows that you believe you are worth the space you occupy and are not afraid of being where you are. Projecting a calm, collected, self-assured demeanor discourages bullies from engaging with you, and eventually they will target you less and less. Interestingly, this is similar to how you should never splash away in a panic if you are in open water and see a shark nearby. It will perceive you as prey and immediately start chasing after you and trying to attack you. Instead, if your proximity to the shark is too close, it's best to face the shark, give it eye contact, and pat it on top of its head as you swim away. That gesture makes the shark believe that you are also a predator and not prey it can easily attack. People are the same. Once you show them that you are afraid of them, they can use it to their advantage. Stay strong and practice being composed until it becomes your default reflex!

- **Don't blame yourself or internalize their negative comments:**

Bullies feel empowered when they see that you are taking to heart their negative and demeaning words. This shows them that they are having their desired effect on you and encourages them to keep doing the same thing. They like to see you take the blame and second-guess yourself. As you work hard to overcome the challenges bullying has brought into your life, it's also important to hold the bullies accountable for their actions rather than staying quiet and letting them get away with their behavior. If there is something you can learn from the experience, it's to adopt a growth mindset and use your experiences to grow, but this doesn't mean you should blame yourself. Remember that bullies often project their negative feelings about themselves onto others, so the things they say about you are not true and are intended to make you feel bad or embarrassed. Do your best to rise above their words and not take them to heart.

- **Mirror work:**

In the previous chapter, we talked about how mirror work is incredible for helping you develop self-compassion and self-acceptance. It can help you get in touch with your true self and appreciate yourself for who you are. It's also an excellent grounding technique, which means that it helps you recognize what is true and important to *you*, allowing you to disregard others' negativity. This is important because the more you recognize these things about yourself, the less likely you are to internalize or be affected by other peoples' opinions of you. Bullies are only as powerful as we allow them to be, so the moment you begin believing in yourself, you begin to take that power away from them.

- **Shine your light even more brightly when bullies want you to back down:**

Bullies like to bring others down or dim their lights, making them feel bad about things the bully is jealous of or doesn't understand. They may be intimidated by or envious of your talent, successes, appearance, relationships, or something else. They might have seen the light in you, and if their light isn't shining, yours makes them feel bad about themself—but that is not your problem. It won't do you any good to downplay yourself or your achievements, and it's not your responsibility to do so in order to make others feel better. If you do begin to hide the things about you that you should be proud of, this may even encourage the bullies because they will see that they are affecting you the way they want to. Never be afraid to shine your light, and shine it even more when you see bullies coming after you for it. Remind yourself that you are special and worthy of peace and happiness; owning this will show the bullies that they have no power over you and give you the freedom to live as you want to live.

In this chapter, we have talked about what it takes to overcome bullying. Facing bullying head-on while continuing to work to improve your confidence and sense of identity is the first step to lessening the impact of this devastating experience on your life. Remember—you have the power and ability to stand up for yourself and what you believe in, and you are worthy of living a life full of happiness.

In the next chapter, we will dig into the importance of building a healthy identity and not letting the pressures of social media influence how you feel about yourself. Social media is a big part of many teens' lives, so we'll talk about how to let it be a positive thing in your life and keep it from being something that brings you down.

5

LIKES, FOLLOWERS, AND THE SEARCH FOR VALIDATION

SOCIAL MEDIA AND TEENAGE IDENTITY

One of the biggest traps we fall into as women is the comparison trap, the "she's got it all" trap, the "she has more fans" trap, or the "she's making more money" trap. We tend to stack ourselves up against everyone else and pick ourselves apart based on what other people are doing. This practice does nothing to make us better.

— ALWILL LEYBY CARA

Social media has changed the world we live in and has been a blessing for many as it allows for countless opportunities for growth and bettering one's quality of life. For teens, social connections are often one of the most important things in their lives and the friendships we enjoy as teenagers provide us with so many lasting memories. Social media allows teens to engage in social interactions from almost anywhere, but social media can also cause many issues in their lives. You may experience cyberbullying, as we discussed in the previous chapter, you may come across false or misleading information, or feel the pressure to get as many followers and "likes" as possible. Instead of using social media as a tool to grow personally or learn new things, it can become a source of negativity if you feel that everyone is living their best life except you. Social media is known to portray unrealistic lifestyles and beauty standards, which can affect teens' self-esteem and feelings of worth. Many teens have a lot of online friends they have never met face-to-face, and though this is a wonderful way to build genuine connections and friendships, it doesn't always meet our needs for deep, intimate connections and can even lead to unsafe situations. Unfortunately, many teens equate their self-worth with how many followers, views, or likes their social media profiles and posts get, and if those numbers are "too low," teens may begin feeling bad about themselves, especially if their friends or classmates seem to get more followers and likes than they do.

Though it can be challenging, you should not base your self-worth on what is happening on social media. It may seem like having a thriving social media presence is a good reason to have confidence and feel good about yourself, but this is actually not a reliable source of self-confidence. Things are constantly changing on social media; follower counts go up and down, some posts get more likes and views than others, and there will always be other social media users who have more of these things than others. Allowing social media to influence your feelings of worth can bring you down and defeat all of the hard work you are doing to increase your self-esteem and improve your confidence. You are worth more than any number of followers and likes, and it's important to keep this in mind if you are a regular user of social media.

There is good news though! It is possible to use social media to enjoy your friendships. By being mindful of how you use social media and aware of the possibility of negativity, you can benefit from using popular apps to keep in touch with your friends. Below is a list of ways social media can be a helpful tool in your life:

- **Using it to stay updated and informed about what's happening in the world and any topics that interest you:**

Social media is filled with interesting content that can help educate young people about various topics. For instance, many videos are very informative and can help young people learn new skills or ways to keep themselves safe in an unpredictable world. We all know there are scammers out there trying to deceive and take advantage of people online, so being aware of this and being educated about what to look out for can help teens be safer online and know how to respond to shady people or situations. In addition, teens can keep up with news about their world and the things they care about, such as current events, movies, music, celebrities, and more. You can even follow pages of people and organizations or groups that interest you so you can stay updated on the latest developments.

- **Using it as a platform to find new and different opportunities:**

Being young is the perfect time to explore your creativity and look for new opportunities to help you find what interests you and grow as an individual. Social media can be an excellent tool to help you connect with others and find those opportunities. You can use some platforms to search for part-time job openings you might be interested in, and you can find local pages or groups if you want to become more involved in your community and help those in need. You can find people, groups, organizations, and pages dedicated to every possible topic of interest that allow you to connect with others with similar interests including things like fashion, musical artists, entrepreneurship, book series, writing, movies and TV shows, and so much more.

- **Connecting with others:**

In a world where loneliness can easily set in and even affect your self-esteem, social media has become invaluable in allowing people to connect with anyone across the world. As humans, we thrive when we are socially connected and have meaningful relationships around us. It's not always easy to stay in touch physically with people you care about, but social media allows you to stay connected and aware of what's happening in their lives, creating a sense of community and belonging, which helps fill our fundamental human need for connection and security. For teens with illnesses, disabilities, or other circumstances that may limit their in-person interactions, social media can provide a way for them to have an active social life instead of being isolated due to certain constraints. This, in turn, promotes good mental well-being and social development.

On the other hand, if social media is not used with caution or is not monitored well, you may quickly find yourself dealing with challenges and negativity. Here are some common reasons why social media can be tricky for teens to use safely and responsibly:

- **Cyberbullying:**

This is by far one of the most painful things that can happen to anyone using social media. As we discussed earlier, cyberbullying involves other people bullying you with threatening, insulting, or harmful language or malicious content meant to embarrass, intimidate, or humiliate you in the presence of a large online audience. Many bullies find social media to be a convenient platform for hurting someone because they can easily hide behind their screens and rarely have to face the consequences of their actions. This is why it's important to find ways to secure your account and be mindful about what you post online so that it doesn't end up being used against you. Some teens may engage in an unsafe practice known as "sexting," and if personal images are shared during this practice, the sender has no more control over where those images end up. There have been too many occurrences of these very private images being shared with the purpose of hurting the sender. Teens also get snared into sharing or posting private information about their personal lives, which can also be used against them. Cyberbullying is unfortunately common, but you can protect yourself by keeping personal information and images to yourself, setting any social media accounts you have to private, and being very cautious and intentional about what you post online.

- **Wasting time:**

In a survey conducted about how much time teens spend on social media, 38% of the respondents said the average time teens are on social media is eight hours per day (RR Author, 2022). That is just a rough estimate, of course, because, with the way apps have evolved and are now being designed, teens can easily find themselves bingeing on social media and spending more than eight hours a day on various platforms. That's a lot of time to spend just scrolling and tapping instead of making real-life connections and investing your time in being productive and actively building your future. It can lead to a sedentary lifestyle, which can ultimately cause more issues, such as obesity if minimal physical activity is combined with unhealthy eating habits.

- **Damaging to your self-image:**

Due to the sheer volume of carefully curated, edited, and filtered images and videos posted online, many teens have started to feel as if they aren't pretty or handsome enough, which can cause them to feel insecure about themselves. This unhealthy comparison with unrealistic beauty standards leads to a poor self-image, a lack of confidence, and low self-worth. This can cause teens to spend too much time on making their social media profiles more attractive instead of focusing on school, friendships, sports and activities, and other meaningful goals. Your success in school and even contributions at home become compromised if you begin spending more and more time on your phone instead of interacting with others in the real world. When you are this immersed in your social media life, you may become unaware of those around you, and this can end up damaging your relationships as people begin to feel unappreciated and neglected.

- **Impeding social development:**

Teens who spend most of their social time connecting on social media instead of in real life may struggle when they find themselves in real-life interactions. Interacting digitally is less daunting, but building meaningful relationships requires real-life communication skills. These can only be developed when you spend time with others in real life and learn how to develop your social and emotional intelligence by interacting with them face-to-face. So, although social media might give you a feeling of instant gratification every time you get a notification for a new message, like, or follow request, you might end up struggling to make or maintain relationships in the real world. This can make you feel disconnected, isolated, and unhappy with the quality of your social life.

- **Exposure to inappropriate content:**

One aspect of social media that can be helpful or harmful is that anyone can post anything, and that content is readily available on people's feeds in a matter of seconds. This also means that teens are at risk of being exposed to graphic or inappropriate content that might make them feel uncomfortable or unsafe or make them second-guess their worth and feel like they aren't good enough. For instance, videos and images of men and women who have had a lot of plastic surgery may make teens feel as if this is the only way to look "perfect" and lead them to feel as if their natural attributes and appearance aren't enough. Teens may come across false or misguided information about sex and sexuality, giving them a distorted idea and expectation of how relationships and sex are meant to be. When their relationships don't reflect what they see on social media, they can start to feel less confident and unhappy with themselves, like they are somehow failing. The content you expose yourself to influences your everyday choices. Unknowingly, you may end up replicating certain behaviors that aren't appropriate because of the influence of social media. This shows how social media can interfere with your developing sense of identity and values as you grow up. Instead of looking up to positive role models and defining your own dreams, you may end up striving to live up to some unrealistic ideal you saw online. While using social media is perfectly acceptable, always remember that many people are only posting about their best days or the best moments of their day rather than their full reality. Focus on making yourself happy and going after what you want, and don't worry about what other people are posting.

Having seen the advantages and disadvantages of using social media, it is clear that you have to be very intentional about how you use it so that it can work to your advantage instead of working against you. To that end, let's move on to the next section, where we'll talk about how you can best utilize social media to strengthen your relationship with yourself, as well as your relationships with others.

HOW TO USE SOCIAL MEDIA RESPONSIBLY

Many benefits come with using social media, but if you aren't careful with how you use it, unexpected issues and problems could arise. Thankfully, many apps have the capabilities to restrict and limit who can see your profile and posts, and there are strategies you can use to keep yourself safe and happy online. Below are action steps for how to avoid bullying online to keep you free from stress and help you be productive with your time:

- **Decide on the amount of screen time you will allow for yourself each day:**

Social media is an excellent platform for connecting with others conveniently and getting some time to wind down after a busy day. However, many apps are designed to keep you scrolling or watching as many videos as possible because that's how the owners of those platforms and the content creators earn their money. This is why it's important to be aware of the ways you can get sucked into social media and set a limit for how much time you'll spend online each day. Spending too much time scrolling on social media can negatively affect your productivity and cause you to miss out on chances to have real-life interactions with others and get things done. If you notice that social media is getting in the way of your grades and affecting your focus on what's important, set a daily limit on how much screen time you will permit yourself to have. For instance, having a total of three hours of screen time is a reasonable benchmark to work with, as it provides you with ample time to scroll while still allowing you to engage in real-world activities and interactions.

- **Use social media as a reward for completing your goals:**

One of the most effective ways to get rid of that guilty conscience for spending hours on social media without getting your work done first is to flip it and make social media the prize you will get for getting your work done. This will motivate you to complete your work, like homework or chores, as quickly as possible because when you're done, you can scroll social media to your heart's desire free of guilt! Doing this each day will get you in the habit of attending to your responsibilities efficiently without procrastinating.

- **Block people who behave inappropriately online:**

Choosing your tribe carefully is very important for your mental health and social well-being. You should only follow people who share similar values and interests with you on social media. Sometimes it's best to avoid bad company completely to eliminate any issues. Before accepting anyone to follow your account, first, check out their social media profile to see if this is someone who seems legitimate and like someone you might be friends with in real life. If someone posts something that is hurtful or rude, you can ask them not to do that anymore and hide their post, and if they persist, you can block them. No amount of followers is worth your peace of mind.

- **Think carefully before posting anything:**

Sometimes, we can get so excited about something that's happened in our lives that we don't stop to think about the potential outcomes of posting about those things online. You don't want to open yourself up to ridicule or hurt anyone's feelings by making them feel excluded from a group activity. Take some time to consider what you'll post and what you'll say about it before doing so. If you're having a conflict with someone and want to vent on your social media page, pause before clicking "Post" and think about what might happen if you post your feelings in the heat of the moment. You don't want to make the situation worse, and you certainly don't want more people becoming involved than already are, whether they take your side or not. Try to resolve the conflict in person and keep the drama off social media. A good rule of thumb is to think before you post and consider what might happen and how people might feel if you do share that post.

- **Don't rely on social media to gain validation and attention:**

As we've discussed, using the number of followers or likes you have as a measurement of your worth is inaccurate and could damage your self-esteem. Some teens post online frequently in order to gain more attention, but this can cause some teens to post things that stir up conflict or put them in a vulnerable or unsafe situation. Sometimes, it can be easy to spot those who are desperate for attention and validation. Do your best to avoid being one of those people by being careful and intentional about what you post. You don't need likes and followers to be proud of who you are. Rather than seeking validation from others in the form of likes, give yourself the validation you crave and continue living your life to make yourself happy, fulfill your goals and dreams, and nurture your genuine relationships.

- **Use social media to stay informed and improve your skills:**

There are so many lessons you can learn for free online. As we discussed earlier, you can find these by following pages that create content that you are interested in. For instance, if you are into cooking or baking, fashion, public speaking, volunteering, or something else, you can search for pages and groups that focus on your topics of interest and follow them. By regularly watching videos about those topics, your knowledge and skills will develop, and that, in turn, will boost your abilities and confidence levels.

Escape the Comparison Trap for Good

These days, more people are aware of how social media can be misleading. Have you ever heard someone joking around by saying life is not an Instagram page? Ever wondered what that meant? It's really true; what you see on social media are carefully curated, edited, and filtered images and videos of the highlights of people's lives. But since that's all we usually see on social media, we can forget that that's seldom ever the full reality of people's day-to-day lives. It's an unhealthy and unfair habit to allow your confidence and self-esteem to dwindle because you are comparing your life to what you see others posting on social media.

Whenever someone spends time getting ready and perfecting their look, they're likely going to take pictures and post them online, but that doesn't mean they look that way all day every day. Just like the rest of us, they wake up with bedhead and have lazy days where they just wear sweats too. In reality, it's a very small number of people who are dressed to the nines every single day, and even if they are, it's still not worth your energy to compare yourself to them—your true value and what makes you special come from who you are as an individual and how you treat others. People who treat others well tend to have plenty of genuine fans who feel inspired by their work. Take Selena Gomez, for example. She has one of the most-followed accounts on Instagram, with millions of followers. She stays true to herself despite trolls appearing in her comment section. You, too, can shine your light by embracing your unique self and developing confidence instead of projecting a lifestyle that does not align with your reality. There is already so much pretentiousness and falsity on the internet, and what gives you a unique and appreciated presence is staying true to who you are and showing the world that you accept and love yourself.

Now that we have established that you are valuable, let's find out in the next chapter how you can silence the inner critic that always seems to be trying to bring you down. We all have that negative internal voice, but thankfully, there are time-tested ways you can overcome that criticism and establish a healthy inner voice.

6

QUIET THE INNER CRITIC AND THRIVE

The critical voices in our own heads are far more vicious than what we might hear from the outside. Our "inside critics" have intimate knowledge of us and can zero in on our weakest spots.

— SUSAN ARIEL RAINBOW KENNEDY

Of all the voices that can hold someone back, possibly one of the most powerful is your own inner critic. It's the voice from within that often points out mistakes or flaws and can really do damage to your self-esteem. It's probably the voice you hear more often than any other voice. Whether you are interacting with others or spending time by yourself, the self-talk in your head doesn't take a break. If you find yourself listening to this negative inner voice too much, it might be time to reframe your self-talk so that you begin to hear positive, encouraging, and uplifting messages more than those that can wreak havoc on your confidence.

When learning a new language, everyone starts from scratch, mostly clueless about how to construct a proper sentence and unsure whether they will ever master the language. One way to get there is by taking baby steps, learning one small aspect at a time with consistent practice until you start to get the hang of it. Eventually, you'll be able to communicate effectively, and as your confidence grows, speaking that language will start to feel natural. Before you know it, those small steps have added up to being fluent in a new language. That's the beauty of learning—as long as effort is put in diligently and consistently, nothing is impossible.

This learning process is similar to how we should think of changing the way we speak to ourselves. You may experience negative self-talk frequently or even receive unkind words from others far too often. Maybe you've gotten used to this and have begun to believe the hurtful things you or others say. It's possible that you may even spend so much time thinking about these negative words that it has begun affecting your mood and daily life and is now holding you back from reaching your goals and achieving your fullest potential.

In life, someone will always have something negative to say no matter what you do, but allowing those negative things to shape how you perceive and treat yourself will only bring you down. You can't control what others say and do, but you can control what you say and do, including the way you talk to yourself. Often, people who seem intent on hurting others have experienced pain in their lives and are projecting their negative self-image onto others in perhaps an attempt to not be the only one who feels badly about themselves. For example, people who were raised in a home with a lot of conflict, hurtful comments, or little affection may not know any other way to raise their own children, continuing the cycle of allowing negativity to dictate relationships. In order to break this pattern, parents have to be aware of those tendencies and take intentional steps to change their parenting style in order to raise their own children in a healthier, more positive environment. Simply put, people can only treat others the best they know how, and it isn't always the most ideal way we would want to be treated. Sometimes, when people try to show us love, we may fail to correctly interpret their intentions and end up believing that their actions were meant to harm us. We might even tell ourselves that that's how we *deserve* to be treated. This goes to show that negative self-talk can become so embedded in our minds that it begins to impact not only our self-perception but also how we believe others view us.

Our hearts can carry so much for many years of our lives, and unfortunately, many of us find it easier to remember the negative things someone said to us rather than all of the positive and kind things we've heard from others. Maybe it was an insensitive teacher who made comments in front of your classmates that embarrassed you, an angry parent who yelled abusive words at you, friends who refused to hang with you, or a loved one who constantly passed out destructive criticism. All those hurtful words are stored somewhere in our hearts and memories. As we go through life, we may begin to act in ways that reflect the trauma and damage we incurred from those words. For instance, if you've been called dumb, you may find it easier to give up in school because you believe you won't be able to get good grades, or you may decide that the career you've always wanted to pursue was out of reach because you don't have the intelligence required to do the job. Maybe someone insulted your looks, and you now believe you'll never find love because of your appearance. Negative thoughts and beliefs like these have the power to shape the trajectory of your life, sometimes in ways that can stop you from living the life you want and deserve.

Because of this, it's vital that we work to silence and uproot these negative thoughts and beliefs so that we can live the lives we want. You deserve to be happy, live the life you dream of, and feel good about who you are. And it all starts with how you talk to yourself.

Your thoughts will always influence the direction of your life. If you think positively, you can attract the success and relationships you desire. Even if negative thoughts and self-talk have been taking over your life, you have the power to change those thoughts and alter the way you talk to yourself. Just like you can master a new language through consistent effort, you can also change your self-perception and inner voice in order to start enjoying life. You can learn the language of success and positivity, train your mind to think differently, and empower yourself to build solid confidence and self-esteem.

In the next section, we will look at some practical strategies you can use to begin to silence your inner critic and invite in encouraging and positive thoughts and beliefs.

HOW TO SILENCE YOUR INNER CRITIC AND DEVELOP A NEW VOICE

- **Develop mindfulness about negative self-talk:**

Mindfulness is being aware of your actions, thoughts, and words as well as their impact on you and others. It also involves being aware of what's happening around you and why. Everyone has a communication pattern, and being aware of how you communicate and interpret situations will help you change certain habits and behaviors, especially ones that lead to your inner critic piping up. There are four kinds of negative self-talk— polarizing, filtering, catastrophizing, and personalizing.

- **Recognize that everything is not always black and white:** Polarizing is when you choose to only see things as black or white, as if there is no in-between. For instance, you might view yourself as unintelligent and base this on your struggles in certain subjects in school, but intelligence can be relative to the situation. Maybe you have to work hard to understand new math concepts, but reading and writing are easy for you, and you always seem to do well in those classes. Maybe you think you have no confidence because you have a hard time making small talk with new people, but when you're around close friends, you're outspoken and feel free to be silly and have fun. From these examples, we can see that making blanket statements about who or what you are is often inaccurate.

- **Rewire your mind to appreciate the positive things:** Filtering is when you choose to ignore certain facts and only focus on the negative side of things. For instance, maybe someone compliments your work in art class, but instead of gracefully receiving the compliment, you point out where the paint smudged and the colors ran. In this example, you're ignoring all the positive aspects and only focusing on the negative ones, even if they're much smaller or less significant.

- **Avoid expecting the worst or exaggerating how bad things are:** Catastrophizing is when you choose to look at things in the worst way possible. This habit is one reason people avoid trying new things; they tell themselves all of the bad things that could happen and become convinced that it's not a good idea, limiting themselves when it comes to new opportunities. Catastrophizing is also when things get blown out of proportion. This can cause anxiety, fear, or panic and infringe on someone's peace of mind. For example, you might think to yourself, "Everyone is going to laugh at me because of my outfit," or, "This party is not going to go well, I can feel it. Maybe it's best I don't go." These assumptions and perceptions may actually contribute to an experience being more negative than it might otherwise have been, so choosing to see things positively can, in fact, help those things turn out to be positive and result in the desired outcome, whatever it may be.

- **Don't take things personally:** Personalizing is when someone assumes that if anything goes wrong, it is their fault or that any negativity in a situation is directed at them. For instance, someone might say, "We need to improve our personal hygiene." Instead of viewing this as a general comment, someone who personalizes things may think that the comment was directed at them and even intended as somewhat of an attack. As a result, they might feel sad, embarrassed, or unsure of themselves and concerned that everyone thinks they have bad hygiene.

All of these forms of negative self-talk can be very detrimental to our self-esteem and confidence, which is why practicing mindfulness, especially when it comes to our self-perception and inner voice, and intentionally changing how we talk to ourselves is so important.

- **Talk to yourself the same way you would talk to a friend:**

Often, we speak more kindly to others than we do to ourselves. The irony of this is that people tend to treat us the way we treat ourselves rather than the way we treat them, so no matter how nice and considerate you are toward others, if you are unkind to yourself, you might find others treating you that same way. It's kind of like how babies learn to talk by mimicking the way the adults around them speak: People will learn to talk to you the way you talk to yourself. We subconsciously pick up on others' energy and end up treating others based on the energy they give off. So if you want to be more confident and develop a healthy relationship with yourself and others, start with how you communicate. Your self-talk can lift you up or bring you down, so to start making a change, talk to yourself the way you'd talk to a close friend. Use kindness and love rather than criticism to guide your communication. This will start to increase your self-love and self-esteem and decrease the negative feelings you may have about yourself.

- **Reframe your mindset:**

If you notice that you often have negative thoughts, take some time to understand why rather than getting frustrated with yourself. Everyone is the way they are for a reason. Perhaps you grew up always hearing negative things, and now it is difficult for you to see things differently, or maybe thinking negatively helps you feel prepared for the worst-case scenario. No matter what happened that shaped how you think and talk to yourself today, you are capable of making positive changes to your self-image and mindset. If you have what is known as a "fixed mindset," you may believe that the way you are cannot be changed no matter what you do, but there are steps you can take to develop a growth mindset in which you believe that it is possible to make any changes you want with effort and practice. A growth mindset will allow you to keep growing in many areas, whereas a fixed mindset will keep you stuck where you are with no hope of anything changing and with the belief that you will never be able to do anything you can't already do, which holds you back from reaching your true potential. In order to reframe your thoughts, you have to notice the negative thoughts, purposefully stop them, and change them to something more positive to keep from spiraling downward. It's kind of like changing the channel on TV. If you don't like what is on, you can switch to a different channel. Similarly, when you notice the negative, you can take steps to make the switch to positive. It does take practice, but you have the power to change your mindset.

- **Practice mindfulness:**

Sometimes, our negativity comes from focusing on things that happened in the past that were unpleasant or hurtful. Even if they happened long ago, you may still think about them and allow them to impact your self-esteem. You may even feel stuck in the past and unable to move forward and embrace the present. One way to change this is to use mindfulness to help your mind let go of the past and start being focused on the present. When you are living in the present moment, you are able to create a different reality, but if your mind is often stuck in the past, you might feel like there is no way to change your daily experiences. Practicing mindfulness by taking time to appreciate the present, letting go of things that happened in the past, and using affirmations to remind yourself that you are not who you used to be, will help you recognize the positive things in your life, as well as the areas you can focus on improving without beating yourself up over them. Using deep breathing exercises and practicing mirror work can help you be more self-aware and appreciate how much you've grown as an individual. Whenever you notice your thoughts wandering off to the past, you can say these words out loud: "That was then; now is a different story. I am proud of what I have and who I am today." This will help your mind to be more conscious of the present and less worried about the past.

- **Get a gratitude journal**:

Sometimes, our negative feelings or self-talk come from feeling bad about the things we don't have rather than focusing on all that we do have to be grateful for. Sometimes, we forget to acknowledge how far we've come as we continue striving for new goals, but if you wait to feel good about yourself until you have achieved everything you want, you may end up feeling more dissatisfied than you should. The trick is learning to enjoy and appreciate where you are and what you have while you work on accomplishing your other goals. It's not fair for you to have unrealistic expectations of yourself. You deserve to celebrate and enjoy every single achievement and positive step you take. By doing so, your confidence will grow, and you will project an irresistible energy that will attract others to you. Gratitude is proven to increase happiness, which will help boost your self-esteem and overall satisfaction in life. One way to bring more of this into your life is by getting and regularly using a gratitude journal. In your gratitude journal, you can reflect on the positive things about your life and all of the things you have to be grateful for, both material possessions and otherwise. You might be surprised by how many great things there are in your life. Regularly writing in your gratitude journal will increase your positive self-talk and ultimately help shift your mindset.

- **Actively work on overcoming your weaknesses:**

It's okay to recognize things about yourself you'd like to improve, but if all you ever tell yourself is what's not good enough about you, that can be harmful to your self-esteem. Unfortunately, that is your inner critic's specialty, and that voice can really do some damage if you don't take steps to silence it. It can be so convincing because it often targets the issues you know you struggle with already. For example, if you wish you had better grades, your inner critic may seem to be constantly pointing out when you don't get an A on an assignment, and this can be very discouraging after a while. However, it is possible to positively reframe this; instead of seeing these things as weaknesses or shortcomings, use them to identify areas you'd like to grow in and use them as motivation to do so. When you catch your inner critic getting loud, make a conscious effort to stop those thoughts and instead focus on the steps you can take to overcome challenges or improve in whatever area you want to improve in, whether it be your grades, your health, friendships, or something else. By doing this, you can use your inner critic to help you become a better version of yourself. So next time your inner critic pipes in with negativity, you can turn that into a tool to help you reach your goals.

Take a moment now to reflect on how these tips and strategies can help you develop a positive inner voice and, ultimately, a stronger, healthier relationship with yourself. By changing how you talk to yourself, you are taking the first step toward the life of confidence and positivity you want to live. Your courage to try new things will grow, and you will eventually find yourself experiencing success in more areas of your life. As you commit to embracing positivity every single day, all of the obstacles negative self-talk has put in your way will seem surmountable and begin to fade away. In the next chapter, we will take this idea of positive self-talk even further and start to explore ways that you can start to live your life fearlessly.

7

CONQUERING FEAR AND FINDING FREEDOM

Becoming fearless isn't the point. That's impossible. It's learning how to control your fear, and how to be free from it.

—VERONICA ROTH

Fear is a powerful emotion, and it can stand in the way of your freedom and ability to confidently live your life. As a teen, it's common to experience fears of things like the future and the unknown. In fact, it can be a good thing to have a certain level of fear—this is called healthy fear. People with healthy fears are more likely to avoid dangerous situations and make better choices when it comes to taking risks. For instance, if you are afraid of being expelled from school or not getting into your first-choice college, you'll likely make decisions that won't get you in trouble or that will help you achieve the grades you need to be accepted where you want to go. Perhaps you're afraid of being alone or not having any friends. This kind of fear can lead you to be kind and understanding with your friends and take steps to be a good and trustworthy friend yourself. These examples show us that sometimes fear can motivate us to live the lives we want to live, but it's important to recognize when fear becomes limiting or starts to hold us back and find ways to manage those fears so that we can continue moving forward. In this chapter, we'll discuss how fear works and explore strategies for how you can overcome it.

There are primarily three kinds of fears: primal, irrational, and rational, and it's possible for one fear to fall into more than one of these categories. Primal fears are fears that are ingrained in us as humans and have helped us survive throughout the millennia, such as fears of spiders, heights, enclosed or dark spaces, loud noises, and so on (Karl, 2022). Someone with these kinds of fears may make choices that help them survive or live longer. Irrational fears are fears that don't really make sense, and sometimes you may not even be sure why you have a certain fear. A fear of clowns, needles, or the dentist are examples of irrational fears. In contrast, a rational fear is one that is pretty logical and, like primal fears, can help keep you safe. Rational fears arise when you are faced with an actual threat of something bad happening. For instance, it's logical to be afraid of the aggressive dogs that live down the street if they often escape their yard and come into yours. It makes sense to be afraid of walking alone at night if you live in an unsafe neighborhood. Ultimately, it's important to recognize your fears and be able to manage them so that you can carry on living and enjoying your life.

In addition to the three kinds of fears, there are four major categories that we all face. *Physical fear* is something that makes us feel threatened and unsafe. This may be a fear of heights, a bully, or even speaking in front of an audience. Phobias are an example of extreme physical fear, such as claustrophobia. *Anxiety* is a fear that is focused on the future instead of the present. Anxiety affects 18% of the population in America (Conlon, 2023). It causes difficulty with sleeping and concentrating. Many teens experience social anxiety when they think about being in a social setting, such as a party, likely due to a fear of being judged. *Fear of uncertainty* often prevents us from leaving our comfort zone and achieving our goals. An example of this would be the fear of trying out for a new school sports team. Certainty is one of our most powerful needs. *Fear of failure* can also prevent us from taking risks or trying new things. Failure can make us feel defeated and insignificant. However, it is imperative to realize that failure is a necessary step toward success. When we fail, we learn something and grow from it. We learn what worked and what didn't work. Failure is feedback.

A good place to start when dealing with fear is to ask yourself what it is that you are most afraid of—you might even want to write out a list to help you get your ideas down on paper. After listing all your fears, try to identify any possible reasons for those fears and jot those down as well. Next, make another list or do some freewriting about the life you would like to live if you didn't have to deal with those fears. Brainstorm possible action steps you can take to begin conquering those fears. You might be surprised to realize that you already have the answer to how to overcome many of them. Because these are fears you experience personally, your own ideas for how to work through them will likely be the most effective, but in the next section, we're going to talk about some things you can do to start facing and overcoming your fears.

If you're worried or unsure that you'll be able to overcome any of your fears, that's completely understandable, but remember—you have the power to make the positive changes you want to see in your life. The first step to making those changes is to take action. Doing things differently will help you finally experience what's on the other side of fear.

As we dive further into how fear plays a part in our lives and how you can work through your fears, let's take a look at some wise words about facing them from actor Matthew McConaughey (Taylor, 2020):

Instead of denying those fears, declare them. Say the fear out loud, admit it, give them the credit they deserve. Don't get all macho, and act like they're no big deal. And don't get paralyzed by denying that they exist and therefore abandoning your need [to] overcome them.

10 COMMON SIGNS THAT FEAR MIGHT BE GETTING AHOLD OF YOUR LIFE

1. Not saying "no" when needed and not saying "yes" to opportunities:

Sometimes, we worry that people will stop liking us if we speak our minds or tell them "no" when they want us to say "yes." These kinds of fears may cause you to be overly agreeable and try to please people, even when it's something you don't want to do or think is a bad idea. Another way fear influences our choices and behavior is when we avoid new or challenging opportunities. Instead, we might choose to stay in our rooms, avoid taking risks, and continue to only do the same things we are used to.

2. Trying to control situations or feeling paranoid:

Sometimes, our fears can push us to try and control people or situations because we don't trust that things will work out the way we want them to. Fears may also cause us to feel paranoid; this can be things like worrying that others don't like you or are talking about you behind your back or even feeling that the world is not a safe place. These kinds of fears can hold you back from enjoying life, getting to experience new things, or taking advantage of opportunities.

3. Being indecisive or following others even if it doesn't feel right:

Self-doubt can creep in when you experience fear, and self-doubt can lead you to downplay your abilities or successes and not trust in your own instincts. As a result, you may depend too much on other people's opinions and trust their judgment more than your own by allowing them to make decisions that affect you. This is when you need to take a step back, identify what feels right for you, and trust in your own judgment so you can make the best decisions for yourself.

4. Having physical reactions when you feel excessively stressed, afraid, or worried:

When the mind is constantly in survival mode, the body's immune system is affected, and this can impact your physical health. Physical symptoms like headaches or a racing heart are signs of how much stress is really affecting you and tell you that you may need to make some changes to keep yourself healthy.

5. Being in the habit of settling for less and minimizing your strengths:

Your potential is limitless, but fear can make you believe that you can't do certain things and that if you do decide to take a risk, it will be something you might regret. So if you find yourself downplaying your abilities and talents or experiencing imposter syndrome, this is a sign that you may be letting fear influence your choices. Being afraid of dreaming big, asserting yourself, and advocating for your goals is a common pattern for someone struggling with fear.

6. Artificially filling your time as a way to avoid facing what you have to do:

When we put off doing what we know we need to do, like homework or chores, we often end up feeling guilty. Perhaps we're afraid to jump into what we need to do for one reason or another, but whatever it is, that fear of getting started on things can push us to find other things to fill the time so that we appear busy. You might go shopping, make yourself a snack, call a friend, listen to some music, or scroll social media as a way to put off doing what you need to do, especially if you're afraid it will be challenging or time-consuming. You may even do something helpful or productive as you procrastinate on fulfilling your obligations, but using these things as an excuse to avoid certain things isn't good for your personal development.

7. Procrastinating:

You know you have a big project due soon, but instead of getting started, you tell yourself you have plenty of time. As the due date approaches, you still take comfort in how many days are left until you have to be done, but then all of a sudden, it's the night before it's due, and you haven't even started. Sound familiar? Procrastinating, even when we don't realize that's what we're doing, may be done out of fear—fear of doing something new or hard, fear of not doing it well or not being capable of the required work, or even fear of not understanding what's being asked of you or reaching out for help if you get stuck. When you find yourself procrastinating, recognize what you're doing and ask yourself why. Try using positive affirmations to change your mindset about the task, muster up some courage, and get started! Leaving something to the last minute can cause even more anxiety as time goes on, and you likely won't perform any better if you're rushing to complete something in time.

8. Imagining the worst:

We discussed catastrophizing earlier, and we know that it is something that people who often deal with fear may engage in. Catastrophizing is when you believe the worst possible things will happen in a given scenario. For example, if you have to give a presentation in class, you may fear that you'll look terrible that day, that you'll sound stupid when you speak, that others will judge you as you present, that you'll trip on your way to the front of the classroom, or that you'll forget the speech you practiced. This kind of thinking can prevent you from taking healthy risks, trying something new, or taking advantage of opportunities.

9. Making excuses:

Feeling unsure about your abilities to successfully complete a task may cause you to avoid taking responsibility for it. Because of this fear, you may find yourself coming up with excuses for why you can't take on something new. But, again, this kind of fear can hold you back from new and wonderful things.

10. Frequently ruminating on negative thoughts:

One of the worst ways fear can control us is by trapping us in a cycle of negative thinking. Fear makes you think of all the bad things that might happen if you dare to step out of your comfort zone. It can also cause you to think negatively about others and believe things such as people don't like you or make fun of you behind your back. Whenever you find yourself thinking this way, stop and take a breath, then try to reframe your thoughts more positively.

STEPPING OUT OF FEAR AND INTO FREEDOM

Imagine what life without all of those limiting fears would be like! You'll open up a world of new possibilities and be able to build new and stronger relationships with others as you set aside those fears and step into your newfound confidence and courage. Imagine how happy and fulfilled you'll feel once you move past your fears that may have been keeping you stuck in a life you're not fully satisfied with. Making these positive changes at such a young age will give you the power to take control and build the life you dream of. To get started, let's explore some action steps for developing resilience so that you can face your fears and insecurities with confidence:

- **Be compassionate with yourself:**

Allowing critical self-talk to run wild in your mind, making you feel bad for all the things you are afraid of, only gets in the way of your self-confidence. Try to avoid making self-deprecating jokes or allowing others to point out your fears. When you accept yourself for exactly who you are—fears included—others will follow your lead. Never speak unkindly to yourself because of your fears. Saying things like "I'm such a coward" or "I'm just a loser" won't help you build your confidence or move past your fears. Instead, focus on positive affirmations that will help you overcome your fears. Examples include saying things like "I feel afraid of taking this risk, but I will do it anyway because I will have more respect for myself just for trying" or "I am feeling scared, but I have faith that things will work out, and regardless of the outcome, I know this experience will help me grow."

- **Accept that you will fail:**

Everyone fails! Successful people fail not once but many times. Acknowledging that you will fail on your path toward success makes you less afraid of it. Know that failure is a valuable learning tool that will help you move one step closer to your goal.

- **Be authentic and honest about your struggles:**

Talking about your fears with those close to you, like family and friends, empowers them to help and support you as you work to overcome those fears. People can only help us if we let them. Building walls and putting up a facade to try and protect ourselves often only makes things worse. Try to find someone you can be open and honest with and who will support you in overcoming your fears every step of the way. If you can reach out to someone who can coach or mentor you, even a professional therapist, you'll have guidance you can trust to learn new ways to cope and develop the strength to take on any challenge you face.

- **Focus on the positive to help you overcome fear:**

Looking at the positive side of a situation gives you the strength and tenacity to accept your fears but choose to move forward in spite of them. Visualizing your goal redirects your focus away from your fear and toward your goal. For example, if you meet a new classmate who you'd like to be friends with, focusing on the positive aspects of a new friendship can give you the motivation to move past any fears or doubts you may have and take steps to reach out and connect with that person. On the other hand, focusing on what scares you about approaching a new friend can hold you back from what could end up being a meaningful, long-lasting friendship. This shows us that intentionally creating a positive mindset and envisioning your success can change the course of any situation and maybe your entire life.

- **Recognize small wins one day at a time:**

The more you focus on each small win as it happens, the more those wins will compound over time, and eventually you will notice that what once seemed insurmountable wasn't so hard after all. The fears that once held you back will seem small and insignificant, and you'll be grateful you found the courage to face them. Taking things one step at a time is the way to successfully overcome what may have once seemed impossible. For example, if you have a fear of public speaking, you can start to overcome that fear by volunteering to give answers or share ideas during class or group discussions. You'll start to realize that it's not as scary as you thought, and your confidence will begin to grow. Next, you can join a public speaking club where you can safely practice how to be articulate with others who have a similar interest. Watching movies and trying to imitate how great people talk can also help you improve your speaking skills. Whatever it is, set a goal for what you would like to achieve and take the time to find ways to reach that goal. Preparation and practice for those challenges or goals will lead to great results, and this will ultimately boost your confidence.

- **Start taming your fears by practicing mindfulness:**

Sometimes, the decisions we make are influenced or even dictated by our fears. For example, if you get an invitation to a friend's party or family get-together, your instant reaction might be to decline the invitation and opt to spend that time alone instead. That response is hardwired in your brain from years of doing the same thing. Being mindful of how your fears impact your thinking and observing the way you make choices based on those fears gives you insight into your behavior and is the first step to changing it. After reflecting on this, think carefully about how you will respond to the invitation—or whatever the situation might be—and see whether you can overcome your limiting fear and take a healthy risk to do something new. Consider the root cause of your fear. Is it fear of failure? Fear of uncertainty? Reflecting for a moment before taking action can help you overcome that fear more effectively.

- **Let go of self-doubt and perfectionism:**

We all experience self-doubt at some point in our lives, and some deal with it more than others. Self-doubt is when you feel unsure of yourself and hesitant to take on certain challenges because you think you aren't capable of succeeding. For example, avoiding joining a sports team you're interested in because you feel like you won't be good enough might be an indication of self-doubt. This is when mindfulness comes in handy—recognize that you feel this way and choose to gather the courage to move beyond your fear and try out for the team. You never know until you try! Self-doubt can also arise from the desire to make sure everything is perfect. When you put this kind of pressure on yourself, it can keep you from taking chances because anything less than perfect will disappoint you. The key to overcoming perfectionism is to focus on progress instead. If you make it your goal to just be better than you were before, you're giving yourself the space to try but also continue to get better, and as you do both, your confidence will grow.

- **Seek out the advice and help of people who have conquered the same fears you have:**

There are many people who have already faced the fears you are currently struggling with. These people can help you overcome them with the wisdom they gained from their experience. Reading books, listening to podcasts, sharing your concerns with a teacher or counselor, and having a sit-down with someone who faced similar struggles can equip you with the knowledge and confidence to overcome your fears and maybe even become a mentor to someone else someday. Talking to people who have faced the same struggles also helps you to not feel alone and can revive your hope that if they can overcome this fear, so can you. Allow other people to love and support you; you will be surprised to see how much people appreciate it when you reach out for help. It makes them feel valued and needed, so never be afraid to ask for help. Surround yourself with others who you admire and who will hold you accountable and push you to reach your goals.

Another way to keep yourself motivated along this journey of self-empowerment is to journal your progress as you address and overcome your fears. Don't forget to celebrate each small victory and use your gratitude journal to keep you focused on the positive and working toward improvement. The life you want to live is just on the other side of fear. Remember that you are capable of taking on and overcoming any challenge you may face. You need to look inside yourself as well as around you for the strength, support, confidence, and courage required to conquer those fears and find peace and happiness on the other side. In the last chapter, we will unpack some practical steps you can take to live your life to the fullest!

8

LIVING LIFE TO THE FULLEST

Life is full of beauty. Notice it. Notice the bumble bee, the small child, and the smiling faces. Smell the rain, and feel the wind. Live your life to the fullest potential, and fight for your dreams.

— ASHLEY SMITH

Living in your comfort zone is tempting—it's safe, warm, and predictable. However, it does have a downside—it can start to feel like you're stuck and can't get out. You may start to feel tired and even bored of the same old life. Simply observing life from the sidelines and realizing there's so much more to learn and discover can start to make you feel trapped, and you may even begin to feel some fear of missing out (FOMO). You may spend sleepless nights wondering what's outside your comfort zone, and that can make you feel dissatisfied. If you've found yourself feeling this way, there's good news! It's actually a good thing that you're feeling uncomfortable with comfort and realizing that you can do better and live a more fulfilling life. It's great to be curious about the world and who you really are, but it does require some courage to say goodbye to your comfort zone and step into the unknown.

In this chapter, we'll talk about how you can find that courage and begin living your best life. Some people may be hesitant to take chances and discover their fullest potential because of self-doubt or because they've been listening to other people for too long. Now it's time to set aside any limiting beliefs and silence any negative voices so you can make the changes to become who you were always meant to be.

Self-imposed limits can hold us back from revealing the greatest versions of ourselves if we allow them to control us. These limitations magnify our fears and keep us from realizing the greatness we have inside, and they stand in the way of us being able to take the steps that will change our reality. Outside our fears, a new life awaits us, a life that we dream of. Allowing these self-imposed limits to hold us back can result in missing out on once-in-a-life-time opportunities. For instance, as a teen, you can learn more at school than just in your regular classes. Teams, clubs, social groups, and other activities provide chances to meet new friends, learn about people, and gain prac-tical life skills, allowing you to expand your worldview and grow your abilities. However, if you allow self-doubt to creep in, you may believe none of these things are something you can do, but remember—you're working on silencing that inner critic so you can live a life of adventure, success, and happiness. Avoiding taking risks and trying new things can land you in a place where you feel unfulfilled and your potential is unmet. Thankfully, there are strategies you can use to stop any self-imposed limits from running your life. We'll talk about some of these in the next section.

HOW TO BREAK FREE FROM SELF-IMPOSED LIMITS

Breaking free from self-imposed limits should be part of your new growth mindset and something you should practice throughout your life. Challenging yourself at every opportunity will give you many chances to learn, grow, and contribute to your relationships and society as a whole. You have a purpose and a difference to make in this world. The tips below will help you take those chances and stop holding yourself back:

- **Identify and challenge your fears:**

Making up your mind to face what scares you one step at a time until all your fears are confronted will help you reach your goals. To do this, you first have to commit to facing your fears, then you'll need an action plan for how you will do so. Set time-bound goals for when you will start to address those fears, how you will overcome them, and how you will deal with any obstacles you might face along the way. Prepare carefully for the emotional, mental, and physical challenges.

- **Be open to receiving help from others:**

Chances are that your friends, family, teachers, coaches, and others are willing and able to support you as you start facing your fears and stepping into your newfound confidence. Be open to their constructive feedback and offers to help. Having people you can confide in will provide a sounding board for you to share your thoughts, feelings, and experiences, which can help you process those things and continue moving forward. They can help you stay motivated and focused on your goals, even when you might feel like procrastinating or giving up. Doing it with others by your side will also help you realize that you are not alone. Everyone has something they are dealing with or working toward. Having a support network can help you work through challenges more quickly and confidently than trying to do it alone.

- **Accepting that change is sometimes hard and uncomfortable:**

Our comfort zone is what's familiar to us; it's predictable and gives us a sense of control. However, dreams are not achieved by staying in our comfort zone. That's why, in order for us to achieve success, we have to embrace discomfort. Often discomfort is perceived as a negative thing, but it's within discomfort that growth is possible, and embracing that discomfort will allow us to continue pursuing our goals. Therefore, we have to be okay with being uncomfortable once in a while in order to truly break free from self-imposed limits. Our brains love doing the same things over and over again—that's why rewiring the way we think is an integral part of breaking free from our limitations, and when you've accepted that discomfort is what will help get you there, you'll find much more success for your efforts.

- **Be courageous and focus on taking small steps each day:**

On this new journey toward self-confidence and a life free of fear, it's important to continue taking small steps each day, so try doing at least one thing every day that challenges your limiting beliefs about yourself. For example, if you believe that you don't have the skills to play a certain sport, invite a friend over to give it a try in an environment where you feel free to make mistakes. If you keep this up, eventually, you'll be able to compete more seriously in the sport. This same concept can apply to anything, you just have to find the courage to start.

- **Tell yourself that you are just experimenting:**

Recognizing that each action you take toward trying new things and freeing yourself from whatever holds you back helps you be less critical of yourself when you make mistakes. When we experiment, we know that things might not turn out how we want or even expect them to, so we put less pressure on ourselves to achieve a certain outcome. However, it's always worth the time and effort to do the experiment and see what the results will be because you can't draw any certain conclusions until you do. And even if one of your experiments seems to fail, that doesn't mean you've reached the end of the road. If it's something that's really important to you, reflect on what could possibly be done differently, make some tweaks, and try the experiment again. This is how you can discover hidden talents.

- **Address and reframe your mindset:**

Many of us do not have a flawless thought process; sometimes we see things from a distorted point of view, sometimes our inner critic is particularly loud, or sometimes our mood affects how we think. Remembering this will keep you from digging your heels in when it comes time to reframe your perspective and shift your mindset. Accepting that sometimes your mind paints reality to be what it's not will help you recognize when that negative inner voice is getting louder and when it's time to change your point of view. When it comes to doing what you have always wanted to do, you just have to go for it—don't overthink!

- **Visualize how you want your life to be and chase big goals:**

There are things we avoid putting on our goals list because we convince ourselves that they're out of our reach. The moment you catch yourself thinking this way, remember that this is how self-imposed limits thrive—by believing the negative thoughts in your head that tell you that you can't do something or aren't good enough. You truly can achieve anything you want to do and set your mind to. One way to do so is by looking at how others who have done what you want to do did it—what steps did they take? How did they overcome challenges? Sometimes even laziness can get in the way of us breaking free from those limits. When we dread the amount of work we have to put in to get there, we may decide to return to our comfort zone instead. Push yourself to avoid being set in your ways, explore new interests, have an open mind, and continue to visualize yourself having achieved your dream life. That vivid picture in your mind will inspire you to replicate that vision in reality. What's your vision? Does it reflect your true potential? If not, now is the best time to rewrite it and dare to dream big.

- **Do it now:**

The more we procrastinate confronting our fears, the bigger and scarier they seem, so when you notice that you're putting something off, remind yourself that the best time to do what you have always wanted to do is now. Even if you don't feel prepared, it's better to start slow than not start at all. Remember that you're experimenting and mistakes are a sign of courage and a tool for learning. Take pride in yourself and keep going!

Success is largely determined by your mindset. Embracing a growth mindset sets you up for a life of continual success and progression. You now know how powerful you are, and by choosing to step into that power and let go of your fears, your life will start to take a totally different path. Believe in yourself; at the end of the day, it is what you think of yourself that matters more than other people's opinions.

In the next section, we'll go through some tips and strategies to help you stay focused on progress and growth each day.

HABITS TO HELP YOU LIVE YOUR BEST LIFE

The beauty of life is being able to choose how you will live each day. You have the power to excel and make each day memorable. It's up to you to create a life that you can be proud of. The following habits are a reminder of everyday choices you have to make in order to create the life of your dreams:

- **Mindfully adopt a growth mindset:**

A growth mindset allows you to alter the way you view yourself and to appreciate the fact that people can indeed change. Even though you may struggle with low self-esteem and low confidence, this doesn't have to be your identity forever—you can choose to be whoever you wish to be. Thus, train and allow your mind to accept that each day you are growing and becoming a better version of yourself.

- **Take time to discover who you really are:**

When we aren't sure of who we are, we become vulnerable to other people's ideas of who we are or who they think we should be. Your teenage years are the best time to try many things, and doing so helps you figure out what makes you happy and what's not for you. Practicing mindfulness is one way to feel more grounded in who you are, so try to be aware of whether the way you see yourself is based on other people's opinions or a true reflection of your identity. Refuse to allow other people's perceptions of you to define your reality.

- **Fuel your confidence by focusing on honing your strengths:**

Most people who become billionaires or excel in their area of expertise manage to achieve great levels of success by simply focusing on what they are good at. As you focus on your strengths, your confidence will grow. Give yourself weekly and monthly challenges of how you would like your strengths to grow and improve. This also helps you to achieve your self-actualization and self-esteem needs. When your skills are continuously improving, your confidence level grows simultaneously.

SELF-DISCOVERY

Finding what makes you unique can be daunting. Physiologically, when you are a teen, your brain chemistry isn't as developed as that of an adult, so that's why you might have noticed that the way you process reality is sometimes quite different from the way most adults do. The great news is that there are effective strategies that can help you escape any possible identity crisis and discover what makes you who you are. Let's now dig into some easy-to-apply action steps to kick-start your self-discovery journey:

- **Know your strengths:**

Are you feeling like that's easier said than done? This can be a lifelong journey because our potential as human beings is unlimited. There are some things you can do to discover your strengths. Try out new challenges and notice what others compliment you on and what you find easy to accomplish relatively faster than others. Another suggestion is to keep an open mind and take a Myers–Briggs Type Indicator (MBTI) personality test. This is the 16 personality types test developed by Katharine Cook Briggs and Isabel Briggs Myers that can help you understand how you process information and respond to situations. It also gives you an indication of what your strengths and weaknesses are. Having that awareness equips you with the knowledge you need on how you can improve yourself as well as which careers you would be best suited to.

- **Journaling:**

If you begin journaling regularly, you will start to become aware of the habits, behaviors, and belief systems that make up who you are. This also helps you notice the areas where you have room to grow as well as opportunities for exploring your potential and developing your sense of identity. Using guided journals that give you prompting questions can be helpful in getting you to start writing.

- **Visualize your ideal self and set daily goals to work toward being that person:**

Visualization is a powerful tool to help you become a greater version of yourself. As a teen, who you are isn't fixed; you are at a stage where you are free to grow into whoever you wish to be. To help you define who you want to be, create a list of the good habits you would like to adopt that would reflect the person you want to be. Some examples of those habits might be exercising regularly, complimenting others, spending quality time with family, cleaning your room every week, and getting to bed earlier. Each day, set a goal that can help you become that person one step at a time. Don't forget to enjoy the process!

- **Ask important self-assessment questions:**

In your journal, take some time to explore your answers to important questions like *What makes me happy? What makes me upset? What do my peers and family say my strengths are? What are my shortcomings? What makes me feel safe and loved? What am I passionate about? Who are my role models and why? What are my values? What are my biggest fears and what happened that made me start fearing those things? What do I love about myself and what am I proud of? What am I ashamed of and insecure about? What are my goals and dreams?*

As you answer each of these questions, ideas will pop into your mind about things you can do in order to be happy with who you are. For instance, if you notice that you aren't great at dancing and you feel insecure about that, just being aware of it is actually a good thing. Having an awareness and acceptance of this can help inspire you to join a dance class or invite your friends over to help you learn new moves. All of that is part of the self-discovery journey.

- **Embrace your values:**

We all have values that are unique to us as individuals, and they may be different than someone else's. That's what makes us all different and special in our own ways. Perhaps you notice from your interpersonal relationships that you really value respect because you find yourself feeling angry whenever someone disrespects you. When you realize this, embrace that and allow others to accept you for who you are. Share with the people in your life what matters to you, and this will help them know how to treat and interact with you. Examples of values include things like honesty, loyalty, respect, compassion, integrity, and so much more.

- **Expose yourself to nonfiction and fiction literature:**

The world of literature is an exciting one where you can grow your imagination and get lots of ideas on how you can discover yourself and become different versions of who you want to be. As you read about the characters in the stories, there are some you will relate to, and that can help you understand your own thought processes. Literature stretches your mind, and it allows you to create a vivid picture of the life you want to live and the kind of person you want to be.

- **Join new clubs and engage in your favorite activities:**

As you participate in different things like volunteer group activities, community service, school clubs, or sports, you are able to have experiences that help you get to know yourself better and grow as a person.

- **Label your emotions and feelings:**

Identifying and describing precisely how you feel can help you understand yourself better. Many of our decisions are often guided by our emotional state. Take some time to reflect on how you feel most of the time. If you notice that you often feel down or discouraged, you can try to trace what exactly in your life triggers that emotional state. Once you identify the underlying problem, you can make a conscious decision to redirect your thoughts toward something more positive that will evoke pleasant emotions and allow you to have a happy and positive default emotional state. Remember that emotions come and go, so just because you feel angry sometimes doesn't make you an angry person. At any point, you can choose to control your emotional responses so that they reflect the person you wish to be. The more you practice gaining control of your emotions, the more confident you will be about venturing into new things, as you will know that you can maintain composure. This allows you to embrace many opportunities, which, in turn, will unveil who you really are.

- **Ask people you trust or confide in a therapist:**

Your loved ones and even a therapist can help you discover so much about yourself. Giving others a chance to share their thoughts on how they perceive you can help you see yourself in a different light and inspire you to continue to reach for who you want to be.

Success can be achieved progressively. At times, we may fear taking action because we expect too much from ourselves and then end up feeling overwhelmed and inadequate. Focus on breaking down your big goals into small actionable steps that you can take one at a time. Your daily successes will eventually compound and give you more confidence in yourself. This, in turn, will give you the courage to achieve bigger goals and face greater fears.

You can help other teenagers overcome their issues with self-confidence – and that's going to set them up for a lifetime of success. It's as easy as leaving a review.

Simply by sharing your honest opinion of this book and, if you're up for it, a little of your own story, you'll help other teenagers find the support they're looking for.

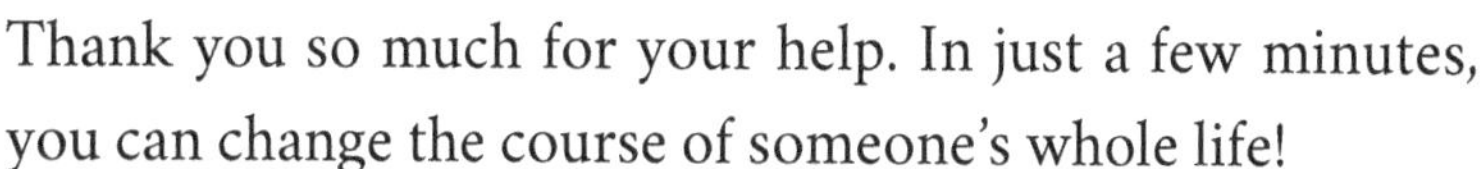

Thank you so much for your help. In just a few minutes, you can change the course of someone's whole life!

Scan the QR code to leave your review on Amazon.

CONCLUSION

Embracing self-confidence and letting go of low self-esteem is one of the greatest and most important journeys you will ever take. By actively putting into practice everything you have learned in this book and in life, you are preparing a strong foundation for your future. Most people who succeeded in their adult years usually began working on themselves when they were teenagers. Your choice to embrace this journey and fight for the life you deserve is one of the most noble and rewarding decisions you will ever make. Out of everything we have learned here, it's most important that you always remember to have a growth mindset because that is how you will be able to close old chapters of your life and open doors to a new reality without having the past lingering and affecting your well-being.

This is your time to develop and reveal the confident version of yourself. I want to congratulate you for loving yourself enough to invest in your personal development. A future filled with peace, thrilling adventures, flourishing relationships, and abounding success in every aspect of your life awaits you. Now it's time for you to go and get the life you deserve—you can do it!

REFERENCES

Ackerman, C. E. (2018, May 23). *What is self-esteem? A psychologist explains.* PositivePsychology.com. https://positivepsychology.com/self-esteem/

Babauta, L. (2022, November 2). *9 tips on how to find passion in life.* LifeHack. https://www.lifehack.org/articles/featured/how-to-find-your-passion.html

Barkley, S. (2023, June 15). *Don't feel good enough? Here's why mirror work might be the answer.* Power of Positivity. https://www.powerofpositiv ity.com/mirror-work-increases-self-respect/

Cherry, K. (2022, October 6). *10 ways to improve your resilience.* Verywell Mind. https://www.verywellmind.com/ways-to-become-more-resilient-2795063

Clarke, J. (2022, June 14). *Reparenting in therapy.* Verywell Mind. https://www.verywellmind.com/reparenting-in-therapy-5226096

Cleveland Clinic. (n.d.). *Fostering a positive self-image.* https://my.cleve landclinic.org/health/articles/12942-fostering-a-positive-self-image

Conlon, D. (2023, May 19). *How to overcome fear: Unlock the psychology of fear and 10 steps to overcome it.* Tony Robbins. https://www.tonyrob bins.com/stories/unleash-the-power/overcoming-fear-in-5-steps/

Daniel, A. (2017, June 28). *How 15 famous men overcame their deepest insecurities.* BestLife. https://bestlifeonline.com/leading-men-conquered-insecurities/

DeSilver, D. (2019, February 26). *The concerns and challenges of being a U.S. teen: What the data show.* Pew Research Center. https://www.pewre search.org/fact-tank/2019/02/26/the-concerns-and-challenges-of-being-a-u-s-teen-what-the-data-show/

Ellis, T. J. (2023, April 28). *7+ celebrities who started out with poor self esteem.* Theo J Ellis. https://theojellis.com/celebrities-with-low-self-esteem/

Escape Games. (2019, October 8). The three types of fear. https://escapegames.ca/three-types-of-fear/

Esther. (2022, June 17). *An actionable guide to self-discovery for teens.* Uncovered Me. https://uncoveredme.life/self-discovery-for-teens/

Feuerman, M. (2022, December 5). *Coping with an insecure attachment style.* Verywell Mind. https://www.verywellmind.com/marriage-inse cure-attachment-style-2303303#:

Flaxington, B. D. (2015, July 16). Teenage insecurities. *Psychology Today.* https://www.psychologytoday.com/intl/blog/understand-other-people/201507/teenage-insecurities

fleetwood-pc. (2019, October 23). *My negative self talk is so bad, it's like having an inner bully and critic at all times* [Online forum post]. Reddit. https://www.reddit.com/r/DecidingToBeBetter/comments/dly1u6/my_negative_self_talk_is_so_bad_its_like_having/

Fran. (2022, May 18). How to build confidence: 5 tips for being more confident. *Future Learn.* https://www.futurelearn.com/info/blog/general/how-to-build-confidence-5-tips-being-more-confident

Gallo, V. (2023, March 3). *10 tips on how to use social media responsibly.* Mind Connections. https://mindconnectionsnyc.com/how-to-use-social-media-responsibly/

GoPeer. (2020, August 28). The importance of having a "growth mindset." Medium. https://blog.gopeer.org/the-importance-of-having-a-growth-mindset-69a0672ab823

Hailey, L. (2022, December 8). *How to set boundaries: 5 ways to draw the line politely.* Science of People. https://www.scienceofpeople.com/how-to-set-boundaries/

Hanh, T. N. (n.d.). *Thich Nhat Hanh > Quotes > Quotable quote.* https://www.goodreads.com/quotes/728048-to-be-beautiful-means-to-be-yourself-you-don-t-need-to

Hasa. (2020, November 9). *What is the difference between arrogance and confidence.* Pediaa. https://pediaa.com/what-is-the-difference-between-arrogance-and-confidence/

Holland, E. (2019, February 26). Why we compare ourselves on social media and how to stop. *Tiny Buddha.* https://tinybuddha.com/blog/why-compare-others-social-media-how-to-stop/

Kapoor, P. (2021, February 17). *6 simple ways to push yourself beyond your limits.* Youth Incorporated. https://youthincmag.com/6-simple-ways-to-push-yourself-beyond-your-limits

Karl, B. (2022, October 2). *Three types of fears in humans*. Medium. https://medium.com/illumination-curated/three-types-of-fear-in-humans-7868e237b7f

Lewis, R. (2021, January 22). *Types of bullying your child may be facing in school*. Healthline. https://www.healthline.com/health/childrens-health/types-of-bullying

Liles, Maryn. "101 Uplifting Confidence Quotes for Days You're Struggling with Low Self-Esteem." Parade.com. Last modified October 10, 2022. https://parade.com/989608/marynliles/confidence-quotes/

Markway, B. (2018, December 7). 5 reasons people have low self-confidence. *Psychology Today*. https://www.psychologytoday.com/intl/blog/shyness-is-nice/201812/5-reasons-people-have-low-self-confidence

Michael, J. (2016, August 22). *How to identify your strengths and weaknesses*. Bplans. https://articles.bplans.com/how-to-identify-your-strengths-and-weaknesses/

Mort, S. (2021, June 8). Confidence vs self-esteem—What's the difference? *Dr Soph*. https://drsoph.com/blog/confidence-vs-self-esteem-whats-the-difference

Moulder, H. (2022, July 6). How to set goals for building self-confidence & fulfillment. *Course Correction Coaching*. https://www.coursecorrectioncoaching.com/how-to-set-goals-for-building-self-confidence-and-fulfillment/

Peale, N. V. (n.d.). *Norman Vincent Peale quotes*. BrainyQuote. https://www.brainyquote.com/quotes/norman_vincent_peale_132560

Popular quotes. (n.d.). Goodreads. https://www.goodreads.com/quotes/

Reynolds, N. (2022, January 27). *Teach your teen to have a growth mindset: Why it matters and powerful strategies that work*. Raising Teens Today. https://raisingteenstoday.com/teach-growth-mindset-to-your-teen/

Rittenhouse, M. (2020, October 26). Body image and self-compassion. *Eating Disorder Hope*. https://www.eatingdisorderhope.com/blog/body-image-self-compassion

RR Author. (2022, August 18). *Over 38% say teenagers spend more than 8 hours on social media daily*. Real Research Media. https://realresearcher.com/media/over-38-percent-say-teenagers-spend-more-than-8-hours-on-social-media-daily/

Sales, M. (2018, October 8). *5 obstacles to confidence and how to overcome them all*. Business Woman Media. https://www.thebusinesswoman media.com/5-obstacles-confidence-overcome/

Salzberg, S. (n.d.). *Sharon Salzberg > Quotes > Quotable quote*. Goodreads. https://www.goodreads.com/quotes/259-you-yourself-as-much-as-anybody-in-the-entire-universe

Schembra, C. (2021, May 6). How to turn fear into gratitude. *Rolling Stone*. https://www.rollingstone.com/culture-council/articles/turn-fear-into-gratitude-1162344

Scott, E. (2022, May 24). *The toxic effects of negative self-talk*. Verywell Mind. https://www.verywellmind.com/negative-self-talk-and-how-it-affects-us-4161304

Scott, S. (2023, April 26). *67 positive affirmations for teens & young students*. Happier Human. https://www.happierhuman.com/positive-affirma tions-teens/

Soken-Huberty, E. (2023, July 22). 15 reasons why confidence is important. *Open Education Online*. https://openeducationonline.com/maga zine/reasons-why-confidence-is-important/

Taylor, R. (2020, January 25). Matthew McConaughey motivational speech transcript. *Rev*. https://www.rev.com/blog/transcripts/matthew-mcconaughey-motivational-speech-transcript

University of South Florida. (n.d.). *What is self-confidence?* University of South Florida Counseling Center. https://www.usf.edu/student-affairs/counseling-center/top-concerns/what-is-self-confi dence.aspx

Vinney, C. (2021, November 8). *What are the different types of bullying?* Verywell Mind. https://www.verywellmind.com/what-are-the-differ ent-types-of-bullying-5207717

Web Desk. (2023, May 10). *Priyanka Chopra bullied in school, recalls "nasty" racial slurs*. The News International. https://www.thenews.com.pk/latest/1068987-priyanka-chopra-bullied-in-school-recalls-nasty-racial-slurs

Yagoda, M. (2022, November 11). Shawn Mendes, Lady Gaga & more stars who've open up about the bullying they faced as kids. *People*. https://people.com/celebrity/celebrities-who-were-bullied-as-kids/

Yardley, T. (2021, May 26). How to stop limiting yourself and feel fully alive. *Tiny Buddha*. https://tinybuddha.com/blog/stop-limiting-your self-feel-fully-alive/

165

www.ingramcontent.com/pod-product-compliance
Lightning Source LLC
Chambersburg PA
CBHW071747150726
47998CB00005B/1843